Windows into Heaven

For the glory
of God!
Kara

Windows into Heaven

at St. Mary Byzantine Catholic Church

KAY ZEKANY

Divine Press

Windows into Heaven At St. Mary Byzantine Catholic Church
Kay Zekany

Photographs are by Todd B. Acker (Acker Photography Studio), Bill Gordon (Photomaker Studios), and Jose Nogueras. All rights reserved.
Divine Press, Port Clinton, OH
Library of Congress Control Number: 2015908837
ISBN - 1512369950
ISBN 13: 9781512369953
CreateSpace Independent Publishing Platform
North Charleston, South Carolina

Contents

List of Illustrations vii

Preface ix

Introduction xiii

Chapter 1   Main Level Icons 1

Chapter 2   Upper Level Icons 27

Chapter 3   Icons on the Walls 63

Conclusion 91

Appendix 1: Writing Icons 95

Appendix 2: History of St. Mary 97

Appendix 3: Icon Dedications 99

Appendix 4: Glossary 101

Appendix 5: Further Readings on this Subject 103

Appendix 6: About the Author 105

List of Illustrations

Image01 – My Wedding Picture xvii

Image02 – Christ the Teacher. 2

Image03 – Blessed Virgin Mary with the Child Jesus. 6

Image04 – The Holy Deacon Phillip 8

Image05 – The Holy Deacon and Protomartyr Stephen. 10

Image06 –The Holy John, Forerunner of the Lord. 12

Image07 – Our Holy Father Nicholas the Wonderworker 14

Image08 – The Risen Christ (Easter or Pascha) 16

Image09 – Nativity of Christ (December 25) 20

Image10 – The Royal Doors 24

Image11 – Nativity of Mary (September 8) .28

Image12 – Entrance of the Theotokos into
the Temple (November 21) 32

Image13 – The Annunciation (March 25) 34

Image14 – The Presentation of the Lord (February 2). 36

Image15 – The Theophany of the Lord (January 6) 38

Image16 – The Transfiguration of the Lord (August 6) 40

Image17 – The Entrance into Jerusalem (Palm Sunday) 42

Image18 - The Mystical Supper (Lords' Supper) 44

Image19 – Leonardo da Vinci's Last Supper 44

Image20 – The Crucifixion of the Lord (Good Friday) 48

Image21 – The Ascension of the Lord
(40 days after Easter (Pascha)). .52

Image22 – The Descent of the Holy Spirit (Pentecost) 54

Image23 – The Dormition of the Theotokos (August 15) 56
Image24 – The Protection of the Theotokos (October 1) 60
Image25 – Our Lady of the Sign (Platytera) 64
Image26 – The Holy Trinity 66
Image27 – Extreme Humility 70
Image28 – Christ the Pantocrator (Christ the Judge) 74
Image29 – Asymmetric Pantocrator Facial Expressions 76
Image30 – The Call of St. Andrew 78
Image31 – Martyred Byzantine Catholic Bishops 80
Image32 – The Myrrh Bearing Women 84
Image33 – Second Dormition of the Theotokos 88
Image34 – Dormition of the Theotokos Thumbnail. 89
Image35 – Author Photo. 105

Preface

This book offers an introduction to Christian icons based on the icons adorning the interior of St. Mary Byzantine Catholic Church in Marblehead, Ohio which was built by my father, Andy Zekany, Jr., [1922-2011] along with his crew of men at Mosser Construction. The purpose of this book is to pay tribute to this wonderful man who was a lifelong member of this church. In doing so, I also share these icons with you hoping they will uplift your soul, as they have mine.

St. Mary parish is located at the edge of a limestone peninsula which juts out into Lake Erie to separate the lake from the Sandusky Bay. At the tip of the peninsula sits the Marblehead Lighthouse, the oldest continuously operating lighthouse on the Great Lakes. Adjacent to the lighthouse property sits the property of St. Mary, complete with a popular social hall overlooking the lake with spacious lakefront grounds and, of course, the beautiful church.

The Byzantine Catholic faith is part of what Pope John Paul II called the "Eastern Lung" of the Catholic Church. While far smaller than the Roman Catholic "Western Lung," the "Eastern Lung" is deeply rooted in the ancient teachings. As the Roman Catholic Rite modernized its traditions over the centuries, the Eastern Rites were frequently too isolated to learn of the modernizations and kept to the traditions of their ancestors. In terms of the teachings and rituals, the Eastern Rites of the Catholic Church (which are fully under the Pope) are closely aligned to those of the Orthodox Churches (which are not) based on their shared ancient traditions.

Having personally been a member of several Roman Catholic parishes and this one Byzantine Catholic parish, I truly love both "lungs" of the Catholic Church. But, the Byzantine Icons are singular in their ability to draw me in and "speak to me" in silence.

My intrigue with icons started after I moved away from my "home" church. Upon returning to St. Mary for holidays, these icons caught my eye in a way different than other Christian images. I wasn't quite sure if I liked them. Even though they are brilliantly colored and richly adorned with gold, they felt unsettling to me, perhaps even haunting.

My intrigue grew as I returned to St. Mary for the Sunday liturgy (our term for our weekly church service) after I purchased a weekender condo at the lake and was able to accompany my father to church each Sunday. I would sit in church, at times, wondering what the icons meant – really meant. At some point during my father's last year on Earth, I felt compelled to take the time to study these icons in order to both learn their meaning and share their meaning with readers like you as a tribute to his legacy. Along the way, I learned their true beauty in the stories they have to tell.

In preparation for this book, I began to study early Christian writings, Orthodox Christian works and Byzantine Iconography; I even learned to paint icons myself. And I prayed and meditated with these specific images. So now, I write this book with my mind, my heart and my soul in hopes that you will pay far more attention to the icons in this book than my words to permit these Icons to lead you to eternal splendor.

These icons represent a beautiful example of traditional iconography handed down through the generations used for liturgical purposes and for contemplating Christian teachings to enhance faith formation. These "windows into Heaven" represent a visual telling of our Christian faith designed to touch our very souls and to serve as a great source of inspiration. We do not worship icons, but we do venerate them and use them to contemplate and communicate with God, the angels and saints.

They give a glimpse of Heaven itself – just as a window permits us a peek at what is just beyond our grasp.

Before I begin the stories behind these icons, I want to take the opportunity to thank those who helped me along the way. Some were anonymous to me as their help came to me when I spoke to strangers about these icons. Others were fellow parishioners, family and friends who had questions on various aspects of these icons or who listened to me tell a story or two about the icons, or suggested further readings for me, or read early versions of my stories.

I would like to especially thank my father Andy Zekany for inspiring me to take up this challenge; and my mother Elinor Zekany for giving me her encouragement. I am deeply grateful to Jane Danchisen Pittman for editing my early manuscripts. Without her attention to detail, the clarity of my writing would be greatly diminished. I would also like to thank Frs. Bryan Eyman, Joe Radvansky and Bob Kelly, iconographer Christine Uveges Loya, my photographers Bill Gordon, Jose Nogueras, and Todd Acker for their significant contributions. I am indebted to all who are helping me through the remainder of the publishing process including Susan Gallagher, Carol Kertis Morgan, Joan Washburn and everyone at St. Mary Byzantine Catholic Church. Thank you all! All remaining errors and omissions are my own fault, for which I ask your forgiveness.

Introduction

As every computer user today knows, an icon is an image used to open a new destination; it is a visual representation of something far more meaningful than the shapes, lines and colors presented on the graphic image. In a manner of speaking, this is exactly what the original icons were and still are. The new destination Christian icons take us toward is far greater than what any digital destination can offer as the icons in this book offer us the keys to eternity in Heaven.

The word, "icon" which is so popular today is indeed rooted in religious iconography. The parallels between the internet and God in terms of being "all seeing and all knowing," are striking indeed, but that is where the similarity ends. The internet may seem to be all-powerful, but its existence is rooted in the here and now on Earth. And, the internet itself is neither good nor evil, but can be used equally well for carrying out both good and evil. Now that I have brought up both good and evil, it is worth noting that the icons teach us the positive ways to live our lives following God's teachings, as brought to us by His son, Jesus Christ. And, this "goodness" and "holiness" is shown in contrast to all the evil and ignorance in this world.

The icons teach us Christ's lessons in color and form in ways that words alone cannot do. The main reason for the visual telling of our faith is due to the fact that a large portion of the early church was illiterate (because there was no free public education at the time). Hence, the best way to ensure that all could come to know our faith was through images: icons.

One of my life mottos is, "life should be divine!" I admit that I first saw this statement in a print advertisement for a luxury item available for sale, but the real meaning of this motto is far deeper. Life *should* be divine! While life rarely *is* truly divine, as an objective to strive for, there is no better way for me to describe my ideal way to live my life. I suspect this world would be a more joyful place to live if everyone adopted this motto.

Religious and philosophical scholars have described my "life should be divine" happiness concept in a variety of ways over the centuries, yet none as beautifully as the icons do because the beauty of these spiritual images touch not only our hearts and minds, but also moves us deep down to our souls – if we let them.

For those icons showing architectural elements, the perspective is far from true. Rather than having a vanishing point off in the distance, the "vanishing point" is intended to pierce our very souls. The buildings in the icons expand, rather than recede, into the horizon. This crazy-looking kind of reverse perspective is not based on mathematical computations; yet is intentional, meant to draw us into the scene to contemplate the holy truths, and not just passively observe them.

Not only are the architectural elements presented in reverse perspective, so too are the proportions of the figures and nature. Notice how slender the icon faces are although the ears are wide-spread and the hair is disproportionately large.

The people are not intended to be human beings, but instead to represent the figures as if in a heavenly form; transfigured by the light of God. Their facial features are emphasized and deemphasized for impact.

You will notice the eyes are unnaturally large. This is because the eyes are windows into the soul. The ears, too, are large (even if only a lobe of an ear is showing). These large ears remind us that the angels and saints are waiting and listening for our prayers, thanksgiving and praise for God. The noses are long and narrow to savor the sweet aroma of Heaven. This also gives them the look of nobility, indicative of their role in the heavenly kingdom. In the style at St. Mary, the height of the figures are elongated to indicate their spiritual transformation.

The physical sizes of the figures in icons do not represent their actual size or "proximity" to the camera. Instead the size represents the importance of each figure in relation to the story each icon tells. In this manner a single icon can represent multiple scenes at once within one overall story to add details in a way which does not detract from the central message.

Some icons show the specific time and place of their setting, but in an abstract manner. For instance, a draped red scarf generally indicates an indoor scene. (Although a draped red scarf could also be used in a clearly outdoor setting to emphasize the holiness of the scene). A single plant may indicate many.

Other icons show the saint or saints on a background of gold leaf. The gold represents the glowing luminosity and wonderful splendor of Heaven. The saints are shown with a gold leaf halo for the same reason and also to depict the inner created light which all saints have: God's light shining through. For this reason you will never see shadows represented in icons.

All icons tell a story and a big part of telling a story is clearly identifying the major participants of the story. Mary and Jesus, because of their importance, have special insignias. Mary, the mother of God is clearly labeled with the Greek letters "MP ΘΥ" which are Mu Rho Theta Upsilon which are abbreviations for Mother and God; that is, the Mother of God or Theotokos, as we reverently refer to her. Jesus' gold halo is also distinctive with the Greek letters, "OWN" which are Omicron Omega Nu inscribed in it proclaiming His divinity, "I am who I am." Jesus Christ is also traditionally labeled "IC XC," or Iota Gamma Chi Gamma, as an abbreviation of the Greek words for Jesus Christ.

Overall, Byzantine Icons are not intended to show life as it was; but instead are written as windows on divinity. Icons attempt to express the inexpressible. How does one possibly express Godliness, Holiness and Heaven from our Earthly perspective? We don't have the words, colors or lines to express such awesome divinity. Yet, our imperfect human attempt to represent divinity expresses our limited view of divinity and is as instructive as our human tools allow.

The icons I write about are all located inside St. Mary church on the iconostasis, or icon screen, at the front of the church and on the adjacent walls. These icons are exceptionally beautiful examples of Byzantine Icons written by the hands of two gifted iconographers: Michael Timothy Loya (who wrote the early icons) and Christine Uveges Loya of Eikona Studios (who wrote the more recent ones).

An icon screen is a typical architectural element in all Eastern Christian Churches. Simple icon screens have only one level of icons; others have two levels as seen here at St. Mary. More elaborate icon screens have three or more levels of intricately decorated icons.

The purpose of the icon screen is to visually separate the altar (or sanctuary), symbolizing Heaven, from the nave of the church (where the people sit and stand), symbolizing Earth. It reminds us of the phrase, "hidden yet revealed," which implies that the true mysteries of Heaven remain hidden to us on Earth even though its splendor is revealed through descriptions and imagery. This age old paradox is visually seen in the Icon of the Transfiguration of the Lord (discussed later) where the Apostles Peter, John and James fall to the ground, unable to comprehend the splendor of the transfigured Jesus talking with Elijah and Moses. The visual benefit of the screen is to provide a structure for displaying a visual telling of important stories of our faith and to serve as a point of reference for meditation and prayer.

To serve as a visual reference for the icons I include my wedding picture, taken from the choir loft. The wedding ceremony at St. Mary is truly special. At one point the bride and groom are crowned as a tangible reminder to always treat each other as royalty. The outside world may not treat us as royalty, but the marriage crowns remind us to treat each other as the King and Queen of our household.

Wedding of Kay Zekany to Daniel Klos, August 11, 1990

The first thing you might notice in this picture is how colorful the church is. It can almost be overwhelming to the eyes of visitors who are used to simple, light-colored churches. Next, your eyes goes right up to the Icon of Jesus the Pantocrator near the peak of the church gable being lifted up by angels. Then your eyes wanders to the other icons, which I will discuss individually in this book.

Starting on the main level of the Icon Screen, we see that the center doors, called the Royal Doors, are flung wide open during the wedding ceremony inviting us to open our hearts to God and to give all in attendance a glimpse of Heaven. From the viewer's perspective, the first Icon to the right (south) of the Royal Doors is Christ the Teacher. To the left of the open doors is The Blessed Virgin Mary presenting her son, Jesus, to us all.

From the center, the next pair of panels are the deacon doors, which the servers use throughout the liturgy. When not in use, the deacon doors are generally kept closed except during Bright Week, the week immediately after Easter, when the Royal Doors and the deacon doors remain open, representing that the gates of Heaven have been opened by the resurrection for all to enter. Our belief is that all who "fall asleep in the Lord" during this week, are assured of immediately entering Heaven because the doors have been opened to all.

The outer most pair of panels of the Iconostasis on the main level are St. John the Baptist and St. Nicholas. Beyond the Icon Screen, but still on the main level are shrines to our two highest Holy Days: Easter and Christmas. Chapter 1 of this book consists of a series of short stories on these main level icons, with the discussion of the Royal Doors at the end the chapter.

Moving on to the upper level of the iconostasis, we see six icons to the right (south) of the center doors which are depicting our six Holy Days devoted to Jesus and six icons to the left (north) depicting our six Holy Days devoted to Mary. The six Holy Days for Jesus are: (a) the Theophany (or Epiphany) of the Lord when John baptized Jesus, (b) the Transfiguration of the Lord at Mount Hermon, (c) the Entrance into Jerusalem on Palm Sunday, (d) the Crucifixion of the Lord on Good Friday, (e) the Ascension of the Lord into Heaven and (f) the Descent of the Holy Spirit to the Apostles on Pentecost. The six Holy Days for Mary are: (a) the birth of Mary, (b) the day Mary entered the Temple to be raised for a holy life devoted to God, (c) the Annunciation when Gabriel asked Mary if she would become the Mother of God, (d) the day Mary and Joseph first took Jesus to the Temple, (e) Mary's deathbed when Jesus escorted her soul up to Heaven (after which her body was assumed into Heaven) and (f) Mary's protection of the 10th century church in

Constantinople (now Istanbul) inviting us to pray to Mary not only at the hour of our deaths, but also when we are in need of protection and guidance.   Above the open Royal Doors is the Icon of the Mystical Supper (also called the Lord's Supper or the Last Supper). The stories of these icons are presented in Chapter 2 in chronological order historically, and not in the sequence shown on the Iconostasis.

St. Mary church is also adorned with other icons on the walls. On the semicircular wall in the altar – behind the main altar and above the two side altars – the icons carry foundational messages of our faith. Directly behind the altar is the icon of Mary at the moment she said "Yes" to carrying out God's plan for our salvation, reminding us that God needs our cooperation. To the right (south) is the Icon of Holy Trinity: Father, Son and Holy Spirit, representing hospitality. To the left (north) is the icon of the body of Jesus being lowered from the cross and being placed into the tomb, representing humility. Moving into the Nave, on the wall above the iconostasis is the Icon of Jesus the Pantocrator, Almighty Judge, raised up to the peak of the church: the most important icon in the church, reminding us that God is always watching us.

Eventually, icons will surround the Nave of the church serving as a cloud of witnesses of the Word of God. Presently, we have two icons on the south wall. The first devoted to St. Andrew and the second devoted to the Martyred Bishops of the modern Byzantine Catholic faith. There are also two icons on the north wall devoted to the Dormition of Mary (our church's patron icon) and the Myrrh Bearing Women. Chapter 3 presents the stories of these eight icons, followed by the Conclusion of this book.

One

MAIN LEVEL ICONS

Christ the Teacher

The Icon of Christ the Teacher illustrates one of Jesus' greatest roles on Earth: that of one who teaches us how to live in order to seek eternity in Heaven. Here we see Jesus, dressed as He typically is in icons wearing the red robe of divinity under the blue drape of humanity. There is a gold band attaching the sleeve to the body of the inner robe to signify His kingship. The icon further identifies Jesus by an abbreviation of His name in Greek, IC XC, and with the Greek letters OWN in His halo indicating He, "Is Who He Is."

Jesus is shown seated on a throne, with one hand holding an open book inviting us to learn of Him. His other hand is raised giving us His blessing. Notice how His index and middle fingers are crossed. This indicates His two-in-one nature and also depicts the "X" of the inscription. His thumb, ring and little fingers are pressed together, indicative of the Holy Trinity: Father, Son and Holy Spirit. These three fingers also visually represent the "I", "C" and "C" of His inscription. With this hand gesture, He is blessing us and all who come to Him. This is exactly how priests today hold their hands when they give the blessing.

There is no better way to explain the message of this particular icon than to use Jesus' own words:

> Come to me, all who labor and are heavy laden, and I will give you rest. Take my yoke upon you, and learn from me: for I am gentle and lowly in heart, and you will find rest for your souls. For my yoke is easy, and my burden is light (Matt 11:28-30).

This message brings a two-fold meaning. First, Jesus invites us to bring to Him all the sins which labor in our hearts and souls and weigh us down, for He is here to forgive our sins so we can live on without them to tempt us to sin further. Second, He is also here to teach us how to see our wicked ways and to walk away from them with love and joy to sin no more.

Jesus did not come to teach the 10 Commandments since Moses provided those to the world long before the coming of Christ. Instead,

Christ's teachings go beyond what Moses and the other prophets taught us and can be distilled into nine simple words, "Love one another; even as I have loved you" (John 13:34).

The yoke of love: what could be easier? Well, of course it is very difficult for most of us. The love that Jesus teaches is not the free-love of the flower children of the 1960's. Nor is it the impure passion which is glamorized in the media. Instead it is an altruistic love that inspires Jesus' lessons for us to love our neighbor as ourselves and do good works for one another.

Jesus calls us to love God above all else. He also warns us to not let the delights of the riches of this world crowd out our love for God, nor to let the cares and concerns of our temporary Earthly lives prevent us from enjoying the glorious eternal life in Heaven. He assures us that if we knew how truly wonderful Heaven is, we would surely sell all we own in order to buy entry.

Jesus instructs us how to let the word of God flourish in our lives and to seek God's kingship over us, for true faith in God is extremely powerful and the soul is more important than the body.

Notice how the expression on His face depicts His gentleness. This is hardly the face one would expect to see on a powerful King. Yet it is the face of Jesus: the most powerful man to ever walk this Earth. What an inspiring face this is indeed! Who can resist coming to a man with a face like this?

**Mother of God - Blessed Virgin Mary with the Child
Jesus, Loving-Kindness or Sweet-Kissing**

There is no image more beautiful than a tender, loving mother and child. But Jesus is no ordinary child and Mary is no ordinary mother. Yet, this icon is one we can identify with yet one which is truly divine. This incredibly beautiful icon shows Mary lovingly presenting her son, young Jesus, to the world. Yet, we see a hint of sorrow in her eyes. Jesus is seated in the crook of her left elbow as if He is sitting on a throne. The position of Mary's right hand is indicative of one who is introducing us to someone of honor. This mother's loving sorrow is based on her knowledge of how her son will suffer at His crucifixion. But Jesus is in the here and now: a loving and playful human child with His arm around His mother's neck and nuzzling her cheek. Perhaps He is trying to calm her grief.

The Child Jesus is not depicted as a normal baby – because of course He is not. Instead, He is shown as a small young man, fully developed and full of wisdom.

In life, Mary likely did not wear the rich, bejeweled red robe we see in this image. Yet we see her dressed as royalty because she is truly royal in the spiritual sense. Her inner robe is blue indicating her humanity, and her outer robe is red indicating her love and holy zeal. Red also indicates she is "overshadowed in divinity" by the Holy Spirit. Mary is known as the Theotokos, or Mother of God, in the Eastern Church. There is no higher honor in the church paid to another woman. In icons, Mary is shown with stars on her robe – one on her head and one on each shoulder which is visible indicating her virginity before, during, and after the birth of Christ. Jesus, too, is unmistakable by His halo.

When I look at Mary's face, she is looking right into my eyes. This is because the eyes are windows to the soul. Although I cannot see her soul through her eyes, she touches my soul nonetheless. I feel the emotion of a mother knowing the life of her child will be one of wondrous glory submitting to an unimaginable end. We know all men (and women) are created equal, but this child is both fully human and fully God. How can this be?

The Holy Deacon Phillip

The icons on the two Deacon Doors commemorate two of Christianity's first Deacons: Sts. Phillip and Stephen. As the church in Jerusalem spread, there came a need for the priests to have deacons as assistants. As the Acts of the Apostles (chapters 6 - 9) tells us, Phillip and Stephen were among the first seven men chosen for the task because both were deeply spiritual and prudent men. All seven original Deacons were commissioned to their roles for the church by the Apostles praying over them and imposing hands on them.

Both Deacons in our icons are dressed as Deacons might have been dressed in the first century and both are shown swinging censers which create two important elements in the Byzantine Catholic Church: the ritual aroma of our liturgical services and the rhythmical ringing of the bells of the censers. While the censers in these icons show four bells, censers actually have twelve bells to remind us of the twelve disciples. The smoke of the incense represents the prayers of the saints rising up toward Heaven. The censers are filled with incense typically by the altar servers several times during the liturgy and given to either the Deacon, if in attendance, or the Priest who swings the censer to "cense" the icons, the church, and the Eucharist.

St. Phillip, shown on the South Deacon Door, was able to perform great miracles, as were many other biblical saints. Perhaps all faithful Christians are able to perform miracles through the Holy Spirit and through the saints – if only we knew how and had strong enough faith. Miracles do still occur in Christianity, but we don't seem to recognize them like the people did in Biblical times.

During the first century, there existed magicians who could keep the spectators spellbound. One such magician, named Simon, entertained his audience by claiming he received his amazing powers from the great God. However, once he saw Phillip's miracles and heard his preaching of the kingdom of God and the teaching of Jesus Christ, he quickly repented, was baptized and became a devoted follower of Phillip. Simon's repentance, however, was short-lived. When he observed the Apostles conferring the Holy Spirit through the laying of hands, he became greedy and wanted to buy the power so he could sell it to others! But miracles from God and the receipt of the Holy Spirit are gifts from God which cannot be bought or sold.

The Holy Deacon and Protomartyr Stephen

St. Stephen, shown on the North Deacon Door, was a prominent and successful early Christian leader – so much so that he was challenged in debate by the Jews. As a result Stephen became the first Christian martyr after being falsely accused of speaking blasphemy against Moses and God. He was indeed a powerful speaker filled with faith, wisdom and the Holy Spirit. In his defense, he spoke eloquently, but his sharp criticism of the Jewish high priests who did not accept Jesus as the "Just One" stunned the listening Jews to their hearts.

In their rage, they stoned Stephen to death. Throughout his stoning, Stephen could be heard praying, "Lord Jesus, receive my spirit." His last words were, "Lord, do not hold this sin against them" (Acts 7:59-60). Not even the brutality of his killers could harden his forgiving heart. Even St. Paul, who would later repent and go on to evangelize for Christianity, was among these first persecutors.

This marked the beginning of a great persecution of the early church in Jerusalem. Those in power apparently feared losing their power to Christ our King and His followers.

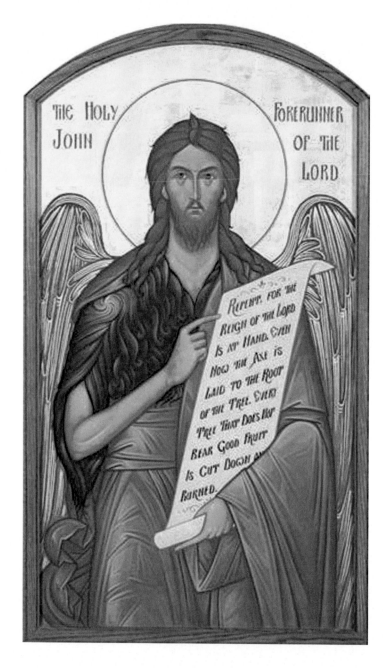

The Holy John, Forerunner of the Lord

St. John the Baptist is the son of Sts. Elizabeth and Zechariah, the aging holy couple who were blessed with their son very late in life. Elizabeth was a cousin of Mary the Mother of Jesus and Zechariah was the High Priest who welcomed the little Virgin Mary to the Temple where she grew up. John is shown here with angel wings because of his role as the divine messenger. Red and gold angel wings are inconsistent with the image of white feathered wings we see so frequently in Western art, but the colors here are significant. Gold on John's wings represents his high status in the Kingdom of Heaven as the one who prepared the way for the coming of Christ. Red indicates John is among the Seraphim (or highest) level of angels. Red also foretells John's martyrdom.

John, in this icon, points us to his unfurled scroll message which summarizes his ministry on Earth, "Repent, for the reign of the Lord is at hand. Even now, the axe is laid to the root of the tree. Every tree that does not produce good fruit is cut down and burned."

John, who had quite a following – many of whom later followed Jesus, was well known in his time for his preaching and baptizing those who repented in the waters of the Jordan River. He did so in preparation for He (Jesus) who would baptize the faithful with the Holy Spirit.

John's robes are not luxurious at all. His hair is long and matted; he wears animal fur under his green robe indicative of his life in the desert. He had no need for the elaborate trimmings of a high priest. Instead, he had his prophetic words. The austerity of his appearance is in keeping with John's message of repentance.

Herod, who had imprisoned John for telling him he should not take his brother's wife as his mistress, did not wish to kill John because people considered him to be a prophet. However Herod had a change of heart after the daughter of his mistress danced at his birthday party to the great delight of his guests. To thank her he offered to give the girl anything she wished as an expression of his gratitude. When the girl asked for John's head on a silver platter, he could not refuse (Matt 14). This is how John was martyred and came to serve as the forerunner of Jesus in Hades to announce that the Son of God was coming to release the righteous from the perils of Hell.

Our Holy Father Nicholas, Wonderworker of Myra

St. Nicholas, the patron saint of the Byzantine Catholic Church in America, is many things to many people and he is beloved by all! Every child over the age of two loves old St. Nick!

In this icon, we see Nicholas on a background of gold leaf. The heavenly gold backdrop allows St. Nicholas to communicate with us eternally in the present, free from the time and space of the 4th century when he actually walked on Earth. We would know this is an icon of Nicholas even if his name was not inscribed on the icon based on his receding hair line, white curly hair and a short full beard. Nicholas is shown wearing a beautiful robe with a draped omophorion, embroidered with crosses, and holding a Gospel Book to indicate he is a Greek Bishop.

As for being a wonderworker, it is said that Nicholas was given these miraculous powers by God ... both in life and after death. In life, at one point, he traveled on the sea through a terrible storm. The sailors all thought they were doomed. But, through his prayers, Nicholas calmed the sea for their safe passage to save them all. News of this miracle was said to precede them to their final destination.

There were other miracles attributed to Nicholas saving those who traveled by sea, hence he is also known as the patron saint of sailors and fishermen. I suppose now that our world has invented motors, he could be the patron saint of all who travel in boats. In death, many miracles have been attributed to his intercession.

Now on to the most popular story! Nicholas' wealthy parents died when he was young. But he did not spend his inheritance on himself. Instead, he gave it to others in need. He gave to the poor in secret by tossing bags of coins into open windows. Some of the bags may have landed in stockings at times. At one point, he was said to drop bags of gold down the chimney to avoid getting caught. That began the tradition of Old St. Nick who we all love so much.

The icon of St. Nicholas is depicted far different from the image we know from our American culture. But, either way, the heart and soul of giving to others in secret is the same... whether giving coins, toys, joy, or life itself.

The Risen Christ (The Icon of Easter or Pascha)

This is the icon of Easter when we, at St. Mary, jubilantly proclaim: "Christ is Risen!" " Indeed He is Risen!" Yes, this is the joyous exclamation of this resurrection season! We are so jubilant that we proclaim this message joyfully in several different languages – some of the languages are from our ancestors, and some are from our church forefathers:

In Slovanic: Christos Voskrese! Voistinu Voskrese!
In Hungarian: Krisztus feltámadt! Valóban feltámadt!
In Greek: Christos Anesti! Alithos Anesti!
In Arabic: Al Maseeh Qam! Haqqan Qam!

Exactly as all who died before Him, Christ descended into Hell upon his death. But He did not do so to stay; instead he did so to release the prophets and saints and to break the grip of Hades. He and those he brought with Him have risen from the depth of Hell into the paradise of Heaven! As we sing, "Christ is risen from the dead! By death he trampled death, and to those in the tombs he granted life!" Yes, all the drama of the week before was for the salvation of our souls – _our_ souls. By death, he conquered death! What an incredible act of love – for us – all of us! Perhaps this is the day that inspired the Sunday school song so many of us learned, "Jesus loves me this I know, for the Bible tells me so."

This icon depicts Jesus in flowing garments of gleaming white, draped in a manner to show off his wounds. His feet do not touch the ground below, but instead He is pictured atop a series of tiny clouds, with His entire body surrounded by a blue mandorla depicting the coming together of Heaven on Earth. The mandorla also tells us this is an event no one on Earth actually saw. He is standing with both hands raised in victory, one holding a cross and the other upheld in the position of giving us God's blessing. He is positioned in the center of the icon between the image of a closed tomb and the city of Jerusalem in the distance. The foliage depicts the growth of new shoots of greenery which reinforces this image of a whole new world Jesus made possible for us.

This icon focuses all of our attention on Jesus Himself, with scant details of the setting of his resurrection at the tomb just moments or hours before Mary Magdalene would find His empty tomb.

Some versions of the Risen Christ icon show Jesus pulling Adam, Eve, and all the other saints from Hades. But not at St. Mary Church. Here all our focus is solely on the triumphant Jesus, freeing us all from original sin and eternal condemnation to Hell.

The Nativity of Christ (December 25)

This colorful icon of the Nativity is full of biblical references which reflect the exquisite depth of the full story surrounding the birth of Jesus and foretelling His life, death and legacy. Tiny Jesus is the center of the icon, just as He is at the center of our Christmas celebration. Directly above Jesus at the top of the image is a blue semicircle indicating God in Heaven with the Holy Spirit emanating down upon Jesus. The Holy Trinity – Father, Son and Holy Spirit – is depicted for the first time during the life of Jesus. While neither the Holy Spirit nor God have physical form, they are represented by a star emanating from the blue semicircle. The three stars in the blue semicircle reinforce our understanding that the Trinity reference is indeed intentional.

In the top portion of the icon, immediately after the birth of Jesus, all of Heaven rejoices with the gleaming sky. Notice how the pair of angels on the left have red in their wings, abstractly indicating the highest level of angels, the seraphim, whose primary purpose is to glorify and praise God. The chorus of ten angels to the right of Jesus abstractly represents the cherubim, or second level of angels: both choirs of angels celebrating this day of the coming of our Lord!

In the bottom right corner, shortly after His birth, the shepherds, their sheep and even the plants rejoice! To the left of Mary, later yet, the Three Wise Men follow the Star of Bethlehem to travel to honor Jesus with gold, frankincense and myrrh! Truly surrounding Mary and Jesus, this icon celebrates the awesome mystery of the virgin birth of our Savior as all of God's creatures rejoice!

But, the story of this miracle begins long before. In the bottom left corner before the birth of Jesus, Joseph is being told by the Prophet Isaiah that Mary's child truly *is* the son of God and that he should not be afraid to take her as his wife. Isaiah holds the scripture which details the many ancient scriptural references of the coming Savior which are now coming true. While the grey-haired Joseph is having difficulty accepting the child as the true son of God, as we all might, he accepts God's plan as his own. (This corner of many similar Nativity Icons, although not the one pictured here at St. Mary, shows Joseph talking to Satan himself, disguised as a saintly old man planting seeds of doubt – just as the devil does to all of us at times.)

Despite all of this rejoicing on Heaven and Earth, we also know there were some men on Earth who would not rejoice at the birth of our new King. In the center of this icon, Jesus, is shown lying in a dark cave to show He is the light of the world, in stark contrast to this darkness, which represents all the ignorance and evil existing on Earth. This good versus evil theme in the center of this icon should not be entirely surprising. After all, our Savior was sent to Earth for a clear purpose.

While caves are typical in Bethlehem, the cave in this icon also foretells the tomb where Jesus will be laid after His crucifixion and before His rising. The swaddling represents the burial bindings of Jesus. Christ is laying in a trough which the animals use for feeding, foretelling that He will provide spiritual food for the world.

Mary is shown wrapped in her typical regal red robe with the stars on her head and shoulders, reminding us of her virginity before during and after the birth of Christ. She is resting on a royal red pillow after childbirth, emphasizing the holiness of the setting. Notice that she is the largest figure in this icon signifying she truly is the Mother of God, the Theotokos! This miraculous virgin birth makes <u>her</u> the center of our attention! The story of this icon is all about Mary, and her role in bringing God to humanity! Curiously, Mary is not looking at her new son with love in her eyes, but instead is looking at Joseph off to the corner. While every new mother is a bit worried about her family's future, we know there are many challenges ahead for this holy family.

The donkey next to Jesus is watching our Lord and is the very donkey Mary rode to Bethlehem for the census and the same donkey which will help this family escape to Egypt to keep Jesus safe from Herod's wrath.

We are indeed a part of this Nativity as we share in the amazement of the birth of Jesus two millennia ago which shows all of God's creations celebrating the birth of Jesus. The choirs of angels gives their song. The Heavens give the star to guide the Wise Men. The Wise Men give gold, frankincense and myrrh. The shepherds give their praise. Even the animals share in this joyous occasion. The Earth provides the cave. Humanity gives Mary and Joseph as parents to guide the newborn. And we, through faith, can carry out the message of Jesus.

This icon truly is filled with good news and great joy of the Messiah for all: both wise and simple, old and young, healthy and ill, good and evil, man and woman, rich and poor, powerful and powerless, the educated and uneducated. God and humanity share the miracle of the incarnation.

Glory to God in the highest, and peace on Earth to all!

The Royal Doors

The Royal Doors at St. Mary depict the four authors of the Gospels: Matthew, John, Mark and Luke. All four are dressed in similarly colored robes to present a pleasing composition for the focal point of the iconostasis. Notably, John's robes are special (as shown in the upper right image). All four are holding beautifully jeweled Gospel Books to visually remind us of who they are. Starting at the top left, Matthew's book is closed indicating his book was the first written. To his right, John uses his finger to hold his place in his book indicating the pages he wrote were about events in his life. Beneath both, Mark and Luke are holding writing instruments to indicate they wrote about events – many of which they did not directly witness.

Matthew was the rich publican, or Roman tax collector, before being called to follow Jesus. Roman tax collectors were not paid a salary, but instead were compensated by collecting more from the citizens than they remit to Rome and were known to become greedy and to engage in what we may politely call price gouging in today's world. Because of this practice – and the fact that they were sending the locals' money off to far away Rome, they were despised and considered to be public sinners. But Matthew turned away from his former ways when he met Jesus, and even repaid all he had defrauded four-fold to compensate those he hurt. Just as Matthew turned away from his sinful ways, so can we.

Beloved John, son of Zebedee and brother of James, was at the center of it all. As we will see, he is the Apostle pictured next to Jesus at the Mystical Supper; in the center fallen to the ground after being overcome by the sight of Christ's Transfiguration; along with Christ and Mary at the Crucifixion of the Lord and the Extreme Humility of the Lord. John is also pictured with the other Apostles at the Ascension of the Lord and the Descent of the Holy Spirit. Beloved John took care of Mary as a son would after Jesus died. He is also seen at the foot of Mary, with hands covered in extreme reverence, at the Dormition of the Theotokos. He witnessed it all!

Mark and Luke joined the original Apostles after Jesus' death and resurrection when the task of beginning the Christian faith required more man power to spread the Word of God.

Tradition has it that Mark knew Jesus in life and is said to have been one of the servers at the Wedding in Cana when Jesus performed His first miracle – turning water into wine. Mark is also said to have helped prepare the upper room in Jerusalem for the Mystical Supper. Ultimately, Mark founded the Christian faith in Egypt and is remembered as the first Coptic Christian Bishop.

Luke is known to have been a physician from Antioch in Syria who possessed other talents as well. As an artist, he is credited as being the first iconographer; as an historian, he carefully chronicled the oral history of the life of Jesus. Luke followed Peter for some time before he became a trusted companion and disciple of Paul. As such, Luke remained with Paul until his end. From these experiences, Luke authored of the book of The Acts of the Apostles – oftentimes writing of events he personally participated in or witnessed.

Two

Upper Level Icons

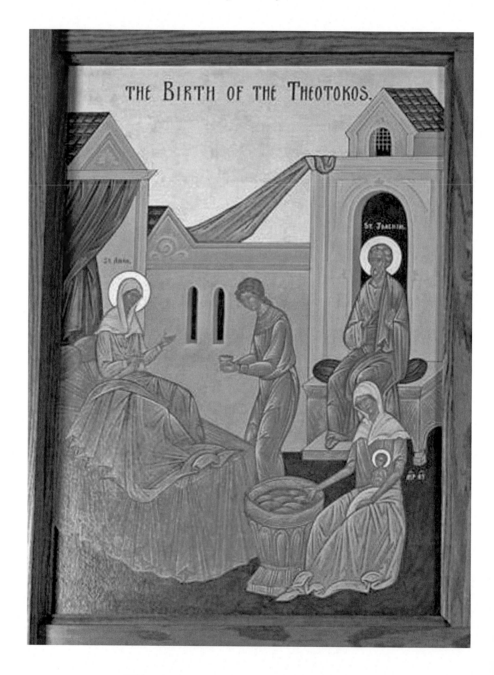

The Birth of the Theotokos (September 8)

Moving up from the major first level icons, we proceed to smaller icons on the upper level representing the twelve feast days plus the Mystical Supper. At this point, it is only logical to tell the story of each icon in historical order, rather than in the order they appear on the icon screen.

The tangible coming of our Lord, although prophesized centuries before, began with the birth of Mary, the Theotokos. Mary's own birth, depicted here, was truly a miracle. Her parents struggled with infertility and felt the pain of childlessness. Sts. Anna and Joachim both prayed to God for the birth of a child. Joachim became so distraught over his inability to father a child that he fled in anguish to the mountain top and prayed for a miracle, leaving Anna to grieve the loss of her husband in addition to her own barrenness. God took mercy on Anna and Joachim and answered their prayers making this scene truly full of joy and marking the transition in their lives from barrenness to full of life! To show their appreciation, Anna and Joachim dedicated their young daughter's life to God. Eastern Christians celebrate the birth of Mary knowing the incredible joy and mercy her son and our God will bring to this world.

The young life of Mary is not recorded in the Bible, but is instead recorded in *The Protoevangelium of James*, also called the *Infancy Gospel of James* or the *Gospel of Mary*, believed to be written in the second century A.D.

The parallels of this scene to the Nativity scene are intentional – as are the differences. The focus of our attention is drawn first to Anna, then to Joachim and then on to the infant Mary. Both Anna and Mary are being tended to by midwives following the birth. Anna is resting in bed and showing her gratitude to God in prayer. Joachim is seated with his gaze toward Anna also in prayer. Mary is given her first bath, reminiscent of the baptism of all Christians to come. With her birth, the salvific splendor of Mary has begun. That is, the birth of Mary set the stage for the coming salvation of Jesus.

Set in Anna's opulent bed-chamber, this icon also shows us that Mary was brought into this world in a comfortable wealthy environment. Mary's life, based on her father's wealth, could have been one of care-free luxury. Yet we know she lived a humble life.

We can tell the scene is indoors by the red scarf draped toward the top of the icon – even though the open sky above appears boundless. The architecture may seem to indicate otherwise, but that is intentional to give the composition the feel of a sanctuary. This scene is truly full of love and gratitude.

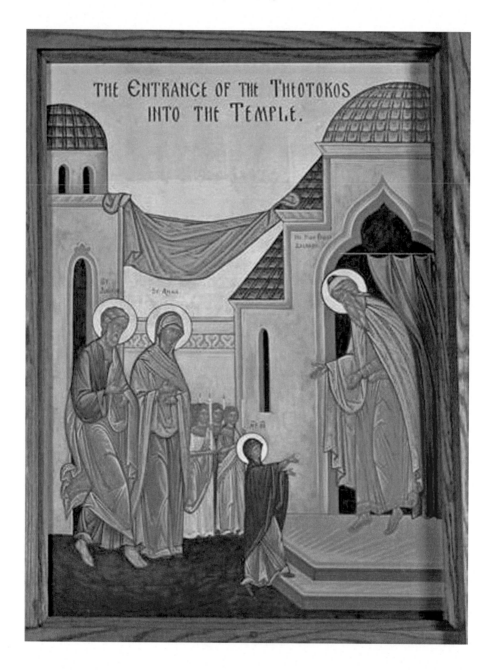

The Entrance of the Theotokos into the Temple (November 21)

Sts. Anna and Joachim did not forget their pledge to devote their daughter's life to the service of God, for which they prepared her for from birth. At the tender age of 3, Anna and Joachim brought their little Virgin Mary to the Temple in Jerusalem to be raised. Wanting her not to look back as she entered the temple, Joachim arranged to have young pure maidens lead Mary to the temple with lanterns burning.

This icon shows the tiny Mary being greeted lovingly into her vocation at the Temple by the High Priest Zacharias. This is the same Zacharias who will later father John the Baptist (although here Zacharias is already shown as being advanced in age). Mary is shown as child-sized, but fully formed as an adult to depict that her spirituality has been formed. Mary joyfully threw herself into the arms of Zacharias indicative of her joy in entering into her role in bringing the light of the Word of God into the world. The young maidens are the witnesses to this marvelous scene, as are Mary's aging parents Anna and Joachim.

Just to think that Anna and Joachim "gave away" their young child – who they had longed for for so long to the Temple to be raised for the Glory of God – is an astonishing act of love for God!

When young Mary reached the holiest altar of the Temple, the Holy of Holies, the Lord God sends grace upon her. In her response, she dances with joy! Yes, she joyfully dedicates herself to God! The feast of the entrance of the Theotokos into the Temple is celebrated as a prelude to Mary giving life to Christ, the Word of God – the birth of whom we will celebrate as Christmas. As we sing in Church on this feast day, God's angels sing, "She is indeed the Heavenly Tabernacle."

This icon asks all of us that God's will be done in our own life just as joyfully as Mary accepts hers. This feast celebrates that God is not only in the Temples; God is indeed a part of the best in all of us.

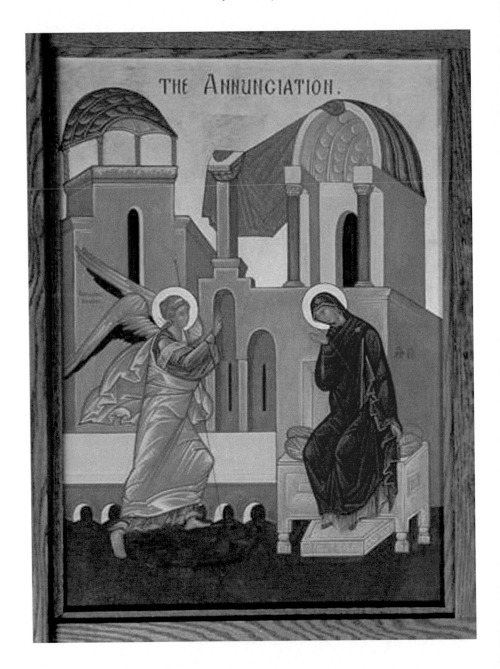

The Annunciation (March 25)

The Icon of the Annunciation depicts the Archangel Gabriel coming to the Virgin Mary as a teenager, betrothed to Joseph, inviting her to become the Mother of God. In this icon Gabriel is joyfully greeting Mary saying, "Hail, full of grace, the Lord is with you!" You can visually see Gabriel almost leaping toward Mary. This must be God's messenger's best assignment imaginable! Yet, you can imagine how confusing this message must have been for Mary. Gabriel explained, "Do not be afraid, Mary, for you have found favor with God. And behold, you will conceive in your womb and bear a son, and you shall call his name Jesus. He will be great, and will be called the Son of the Most High," (Luke 1:28-32).

You can see Mary's gesture as she says, "How can this be, since I have no husband?" Gabriel explains, "The Holy Spirit will come upon you and the power of the Most High will overshadow you; therefore the child to be born will be called holy, the Son of God." In response Mary replied, "Behold, I am the handmaid of the Lord; let it be to me according to your word." (Luke 1:34-38).

Mary's submission to her chosen place in history was needed for it is only through our freewill that God can accomplish great things for the World.

Mary's virgin conception was not the only miraculous conception. Her cousin Elizabeth, in her advanced age, had also miraculously – albeit humanly – conceived a child with Zacharias six months earlier. That child was John the Baptist, forerunner of Christ

Notice how the elaborate Temple architecture with tabernacles enhances this scene. We know this setting is an indoor setting because of the draped red cloth. The windows, arches and columns create a glorious and joyful place for Mary to be praying when the Archangel Gabriel greets her. Notice how the vanishing points of the architectural details are askew and arranged in part to come together in our souls and in part to draw our attention directly to Mary. This juxtaposition baffles the eye as we contemplate this bewildering holy sight.

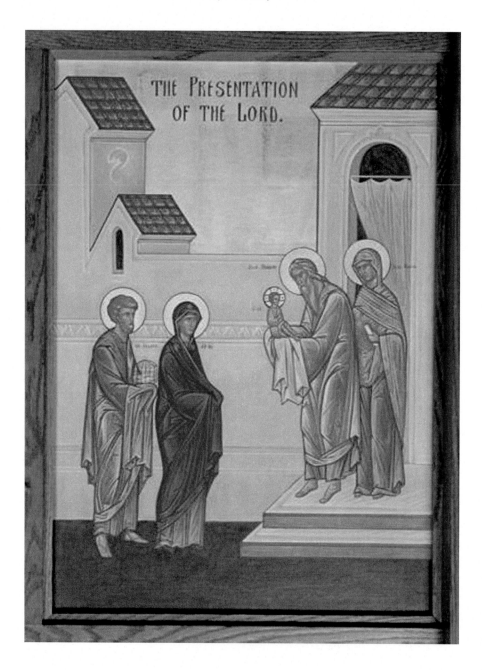

The Presentation of the Lord (February 2)

The Presentation of the Lord Icon celebrates the dedication of Jesus to a life in the service for God. Following the Jewish tradition, the first born is taken to the temple and presented, along with animal sacrifice. With a male child, this takes place on the 40th day of life, coinciding with the purification of the mother following birth. We see that both Mary and Joseph have their hands covered and in the gesture of offering. Joseph carries two turtle doves as an offering which indicates he is poor. Wealthy fathers would have brought a lamb as an offering. Mary is dressed as she typically is in icons wearing her blue inner robe, indicating her humanity; a crimson outer garment, indicating her heavenly royalty; and her three stars, indicating her virginity before, during and after Christ's birth.

In this image, we see that Mary has just handed the infant Jesus to a very elderly saint who shows great respect for the infant. His hands, too, are covered – this time out of respect for the Lord. This gentleman is St. Simeon, a devout religious scholar who had prayed for years to see the Messiah, for which the Holy Spirit had promised to grant before he dies. Recognizing Him, he took Jesus into his arms, and blessed God, and said:

Lord, now let your servant depart in peace, according to your word; for my eyes have seen your salvation which you have prepared in the presence of all peoples, a light of revelation to the Gentiles, and the glory of your people Israel (Luke 2:29-32).

Also witnessing this scene is St. Anna, an 84-year old widow who spent day and night at the temple in prayer. When she saw Jesus she, "gave thanks to God, and spoke of him to all who were looking for the redemption of Jerusalem" (Luke 2: 36-38).

This icon foretells the beginning of Mary's merciful splendor in the public ministry of Jesus.

The Theophany of the Lord (January 6)

The Bible tells us that at this event, the Baptism of Jesus by St. John in the Jordan River, occurred the first manifestation of Father, Son and Holy Spirit (the Holy Trinity)! We see this depicted by the blue semi-circle of Heaven for God, the dove for the Spirit and, of course, Jesus in the river. At this point God says from the Heavens to Jesus, "You are my beloved Son; with you I am well pleased" (Mark 1:11, Luke 3:22). The Nativity Icon of the birth of Jesus, had depicted the Trinity, but this time the Trinity's appearance is based on scripture. Here at Jesus' baptism is the first time the voice of God is heard in the New Testament.

St. John the Baptist, six months older than Jesus, is shown here as he typically is in icons with the long matted brown hair and a full beard. We can even see a bit of animal fur peeking out under his robe – much needed for warmth during the cold nights in the desert. The landscape surrounding the river is shown with craggy desert hills and some vegetation. On the opposite shore of the river we see two angels witnessing the event and reverently offering towels to dry our Lord.

This icon tells a poignant message. Christ our King is shown here in His naked human body ... humbled by the removal of His robes. Clothing not only covers our private parts, but also defines who we are in the world and what we are doing. Here Jesus is clearly showing his humanity – proof positive He is indeed fully human in every visual and tangible way just like any one of us. His feet are firmly set on the ground at the bottom of the river with His feet and ankles interrupting the flow of the river. How ironic it is that Jesus is in the flesh and not covered by clothing ... at the very moment when He is revealed to us to be fully divine and glorious – unveiled by his humanity.

Jesus' disrobing in this icon also foretells that He will be stripped of His clothing, and His humanity, at His crucifixion.

This is the *Theophany* or *Epiphany* celebrated in this icon when Jesus is revealed as merely the incarnation, or avatar, of the One True God!

The Transfiguration of the Lord (August 6)

What an overwhelming sight it must have been when the Apostles Peter, John and James saw the "Majestic Glory" of the transfigured Jesus (2 Peter 1:17)! Jesus had taken the three apostles up to the top of the mountain to pray with him when Jesus' transfiguration took place and, "His face shone like the sun, his garments became white as light" (Matt 17:2). Yes, his clothes became, "glistening, intensely white, as no fuller on earth could bleach them" (Mark 9:3). Jesus was brought into this world to bring light where there was darkness through his words to be a beacon for how we should lead our lives. Is it any wonder that the piece of Heaven Jesus showed to the Apostles on this day is also light-filled? But who could have expected the sight to be so powerful and amazing that it brought all three men down?

When Jesus became transfigured, Moses, representing the Old Testament Law, and Elijah (identified here as Elias, using the Greek form of Elijah), representing the Prophets, came down from Heaven and joined Him on Earth in conversation. The blue circle and the darker blue star indicates the existence of Heaven on Earth. Peter, as an invitation for the heavenly visitors to stay a while spoke, "Lord, it is well that we are here; I will make three booths here, one for Moses and one for Elijah," (Matthew 17:4). But, before he even finished speaking his words, a bright cloud overcame them and the voice of God said, "This is my Son, my Chosen; listen to him!" (Luke 9:35). Then it was just the four of them again.

Wow! What a powerful scene. No theater director could imagine such power! God spoke, some of these same words when John the Baptist baptized Jesus, but without the dramatics of *this* scene. Once this happens, who can forget? But, Jesus implored his Apostles to tell no one of this event until after the "Son of Man," as he called himself, had risen.

The Entrance into Jerusalem (Palm Sunday)

What a triumphant day this icon depicts! The entrance of the Lord into Jerusalem! The crowds were cheering; the townspeople were waving palm branches in celebration and children were laying their own cloaks onto the street so the donkey carrying the most high would not have to place its hooves on the ground! As we sing in church,

> Prepare the festival! Come and with great rejoicing, let us extol Christ. With palms and branches in our hands, let us sing His praises.

> Rejoice, O city of Zion, and dance with joy, O Church of God; for, be hold! Your King comes to you in meekness and humility; the children welcome him and sing: Hosanna in the highest; blest are you, O compassionate Lord; - have mercy on us.

Christ came on a donkey, as a symbol of peace, to make his way from the Mount of Olives (indicated by the mountains on the left) to the city of Jerusalem (depicted by the walled city to the right with the single narrow entrance). Had he ridden a horse, the symbolism would have indicated he was preparing for battle.

Oh how the people loved him as they cried out, "Hosanna in the highest!" They had heard of His great healings and most recently of His rising of Lazarus from the dead after four days in the tomb. He must be the answer to all their woes. He was the new King! The people of all of Jerusalem, so tired of Roman repression, were rejoicing in the streets!

But, the current "royalty" of both the Jewish leadership and the Romans in power did not know what to do. Jesus was winning the people over and if He is the new King, what would become of them? The stage is now set for the beginning of the Holy Week which all Christians observe.

Icon of The Mystical Supper (Lord's Supper)

The Icon of the Mystical Supper, just as the Nativity, is a familiar image … yet, unfamiliar in style. This icon provides a good example of how the style of a Byzantine Icon differs from the Western style of religious art. To illustrate this I will compare the most famous painting of The Last Supper, painted by Leonardo da Vinci, to this icon.

The Last Supper by Leonardo da Vinci

There are many similarities between the two. Both images are Catholic – one from the Western Rite at the Roman Catholic Convent of Santa Maria delle Grazie in Milan, Italy; and the other from the Eastern Rite of the Catholic Church at St. Mary Church. Both images are beautifully illustrated in rich colors (although the image of the Last Supper is darkened with age). Both depict Christ telling the disciples that one of them would betray Him before sunrise.

In both, Jesus is at the center of the composition. In da Vinci's Last Supper Christ is the calm center. In the Mystical Supper Icon, Christ is distinctively telling us of his two-in-one substance – fully human and fully God – with his two fingers resting on the table and by the two strands of short hairs visible at the part in his hair. The Mystical Supper Christ is holding a scroll telling us this passage is taken from scripture. We know da Vinci's image, too, is taken from scripture, but without the visualization of a scroll.

From both, we see how the disciples respond to His message. In da Vinci's Last Supper, we see how the twelve react with different degrees of human emotions including astonishment, anger, disbelief and shock. Yet, the Byzantine Icon depicts prayerful reverence. Notice how the icon is more contemplative encouraging us to reflect on the images to reach a deep-felt soul-touching experience.

As Fr. Joe Radvansky explained to me, both Western and Eastern styles of Christianity strive for the same objective: to bring the people and God together. The difference is in approach – the Western approach is to bring God to the people. Da Vinci's Last Supper shows very natural looking men using very human gestures to indicate their human emotions upon hearing that one among them would betray Christ. We can almost imagine ourselves seated at the table. In this manner, God is brought to us in our own humanity. The Eastern approach is to bring the people to God. We are the *observers* of the Mystical Supper, not the participants. As we contemplate the icon we are drawn into the holy scene. Through our contemplations, we are able to gain insight into *how* to live a holy life. In this way, we begin to learn to rise above our human ways to emulate the ways of those deserving of eternity in Heaven.

Another difference is with the visual perspective. Leonardo da Vinci is world famous for transforming the history of western art with this masterpiece by painting in perfect visual perspective. Notice that items in the foreground are larger than items in the background. We can see how the walls of the upper room angle back to the vanishing point which is on the horizon of the landscape beyond the windows and directly behind the temple of Jesus. In contrast, the icon was written in a style which defies worldly perspective. The details of the room are not realistic, but instead otherworldly. The attempt in the icon is to bring the vanishing point directly into our own souls as we meditate on this image.

Da Vinci's Western style of painting shows the room as it might have actually appeared, complete with a view beyond the windows. Not so in the icon where the only indications this took place indoors are the two red scarfs draped on the columns which indicate this is an indoor scene. We never see an icon painted as if the scene is contained inside the structure of a building. The reason for this is to show the image set in the creation of God – with infinite sky above, and not constrained inside a structure which is the creation of man.

The table in the Western style is rectangular, whereas the table in the icon is round. Da Vince chose a rectangular table for dramatic effect. The symbolism of the icon's round table is hospitality since there is always room for one more around a round table… just like there is always room for one more in Heaven. The table in the Western style is more realistic of how a table may have looked in the 1490s (when it was painted) at the end of a great feast, whereas the table in the icon is set as the first Eucharist, which it was.

Da Vinci's painting depicts Jesus as neither the tallest nor the shortest man at the table, whereas the icon depicts Jesus in a scale slightly larger than his disciples to reinforce His importance.

The disciples are shown dressed in different attire and standing at the table in a different order. In the Icon of the Mystical Supper we recognize Judas with his hand outstretched and dipping into the dish. Toward the left of icon the image, we see one disciple with his gaze directed *away* from Jesus. It is possible this is Doubting Thomas, looking for evidence that Jesus' words are the truth. The disciple to Jesus' left (from the viewer's point of view) may be Peter, in the blue and brown, the rock of the church soon to be formed. Perhaps it is his brother Andrew, in the red and green, who is at his brother's side. The most reverent disciple bowing to Jesus is the Beloved John, dressed fully in red. John's hands are covered as a gesture of offering. This is meant to foretell John's role in caring for Mary, mother of God, who will need someone to care for her after her son's death.

Truly, the Byzantine Icons are designed to tell Biblical stories both for liturgical reasons and for people who are unable to read, as was typical in the poor countryside in much of the Byzantine Empire. While illiteracy was also still common among the poor in Italy in da Vinci's day, The Last Supper painting was meant to be seen by well-educated Catholics who would not need this imagery to tell a story. Thus, da Vinci's masterpiece was for artistic purposes.

The final significant difference is that Icons are written by iconographers who write the icons with divine inspiration to represent Heaven as seen on Earth. In contrast, da Vinci's beautiful religious image was meant for illustration purposes and to showcase Leonardo's magnificent human artistry.

The Crucifixion of the Lord (Good Friday)

What a difference a few days make! It was just Sunday when the people of Jerusalem celebrated their Lord's entry into their city and now on Friday they have crucified Him. It had been a tumultuous week.

The peoples' love for their new Lord on Sunday worried the leaders of Jerusalem as if He would soon surpass their own powers. Then, on Monday He threw out the merchants and money changers from the temple enraging another powerful constituency. Plus His peaceful coming disappointed many who expected swifter changes.

On Tuesday, when Jesus returned to the Temple, the chief priests, scribes and elders questioned Jesus' authority for His actions, but feared arresting Him with the large crowds assembled.

Jesus continued to preach in the Temple that week although he knew how this week would unfold. This brings us to His capture and arrest after the Mystical Supper and his condemnation in the square and ultimately to His crucifixion.

Here He hangs limp with His head slumped onto His shoulder and His body nailed to a cross with a gash in His side. He has breathed his last breath and His mother and beloved Apostle John weep for this indignant end. Here begins the sorrowful splendor of Mary when she was crowned as the mother of all the faithful.

The crucifixion took place just beyond the walled city of Jerusalem with the architecture represented in the typical reverse perspective which gets wider as we move backward instead of narrower and smaller, as we see in other icons.

Above the cross we see the sun and the moon depicted aloft in the clouds representing the eclipse of the sun by the moon as described in scripture.

While the scene appears horrific by its most visible elements, this icon is truly triumphant! Jesus is now conquering death! As we see the skull and bones of Adam below His cross, He is now descending into Hell to save the lost souls! He is about to demonstrate to the world that life does not end at one's human death, but the soul continues on for eternity.

Adam's skull is significant to the meaning of this icon. Adam's original sin of disobeying God by eating the forbidden fruit condemned all born from that point forward to original sin. That is all it took, only one forbidden bite. Similarly, Jesus' single act of submission to His torturous death was enough to save all of us who believe in Him to not perish. Thus, we are no longer born with Adam's original sin. For this reason, Jesus is sometimes referred to as the New Adam.

This icon explains the distinctive three-bar Byzantine Catholic cross. The long middle bar represents the cross beam of the cross used by the Romans. The short top bar represents the initials of the title, "Jesus of Nazareth, King of the Jews," placed above His head to mock Him. The bottom, slanted bar represents the footstool, which became slanted as a result of the shifting weight of Jesus' body. You will notice the footstool board is pointed upward toward the left (from the viewer's perspective). This indicates the true goodness of the man crucified on that side of Jesus (His right side) whom He saves along with the other saints upon His resurrection. There is also a second meaning of the slanted bar which foretells St. Andrew's crucifixion on the "X" shaped cross because he refused to be crucified in the same manner as Jesus.

Through this icon we can all be witnesses to Christ's sacrifice for all mankind. We also can contemplate God's incredible love for mankind by becoming human to proclaim God's message only to be sacrificed to save us all! With this icon we are invited to contemplate this holy mystery of our salvation.

The Ascension of the Lord (40 days after Easter (Pascha))

For forty days after His resurrection on Easter morning, Jesus spent time on Earth, coming and going to speak to the Apostles about the kingdom of God. On the fortieth day, He was taken up to Heaven, escorted by angels, to sit at the right hand of God. This icon depicts this holy ascension of the Lord!

This icon, as are most, is depicted in symmetrical proportions. There are six apostles on the left and six apostles on the right. You may wonder why there are twelve since Judas, one of the original Apostles, betrayed Jesus and lead the authorities to arrest Him. Afterwards, Matthias was chosen to succeed Judas, and hence is depicted among the twelve.

The ever virgin Mary is in the center in upright prayer and flanked by two angels who are looking at the Apostles and pointing upward toward Christ who is ascending into Heaven aloft on a cloud, escorted by two angels.

The backdrop is the landscape near Bethany, with the Mount of Olives off at a distance. Three of the apostles have scrolls in their hands indicating this moment in time is recorded three times in scripture.

Perhaps the Apostle on the left (from the viewer's perspective) with his hand outstretched to Jesus is Peter, as he had done in the Icon of the Transfiguration. Perhaps the Apostle on the right, also with his hand outstretched, is the beloved John. Comparing the faces of the Apostles forty three days earlier in the Mystical Supper Icon, one can imagine the toll this ordeal has taken on some of them. More importantly, we now see that all are pictured as saints. These twelve men followed Jesus as simple holy men, but now, through all they have witnessed and all they learned about the kingdom of God, they have all earned their sainthoods!

The Descent of the Holy Spirit (Pentecost)

On the 50th day after Jesus' resurrection the Apostles and their disciples were all assembled together to celebrate the Jewish holy day of Pentecost. Jesus used this day for the Holy Spirit to descend upon them and to send them forward to begin Christianity because it was a day when all would be gathered together. As scripture tells us:

> Suddenly a sound came from Heaven like the rush of a mighty wind, and it filled all the house where they were sitting. And there appeared to them tongues as of fire, distributed and resting on each one of them. And they were all filled with the Holy Spirit and began to speak in other tongues, as the Spirit gave them utterance (Acts 2: 2-4).

All who heard them speaking heard their words in their own language. What a confusing miracle this must have been! This reminds us of the Tower of Babel, but in reverse. As Genesis, Chapter 2 tells us of how God observed the great tower the people were making and became concerned by what man could accomplish when cooperating as all one people speaking the same language. So, he scattered the languages. Now God wants to unite the world in love, goodness and peace; all men and women need to hear of Him and follow His teachings to accomplish great things.

The Apostles are seated symmetrically in an inverted "U" shape with the top seat empty – reserved for the true spiritual leader of Christianity: Jesus Himself. The Virgin Mary is seated at the heart of the icon, as she is indeed at the heart of Christianity. Thus begins the holy splendor of Mary.

The arrangement of this scene conveys a sense of unity. Yet each Apostle has his own unique characteristics and unique way to bring God's message to the world.

At the bottom of the icon is a King, surrounded by darkness who the Apostles appear to be talking to. This is King Cosmos, shown to represent *us* – all of humanity – living in the darkness and in need of God's message.

The Dormition of the Theotokos (August 15)

The Icon of the Dormition of the Theotokos celebrates the falling asleep of the ever Virgin Mary and the assumption of Mary into Heaven. While celebrating death seems like an oxymoron, this icon tells the hopeful story of salvation for mankind inspiring the Hail Mary Prayer:

> Hail Mary, full of grace, the Lord is with thee; blessed art thou amongst women, and blessed is the fruit of thy womb Jesus. Holy Mary, Mother of God, pray for us sinners now and at the hour of our death. Amen.

This is indeed an icon of hope that our souls will be taken up into the heavenly paradise when our Earthly lives have ended and that our bodies, too, will be resurrected at the second coming of Christ ... just as Christ has done so for Mary beginning the heavenly splendor of Mary.

The bitter sweet story of this icon shows the twelve Apostles miraculously transported back to Jerusalem to surround Mary at the hour of her death. The grief for the end of her Earthly life is evident in the faces of the now aged Apostles and the two Bishops in the room. Among them is the Beloved John at Mary's feet with his hands covered showing his deep respect. We also see Peter censing her body, a body which smells of flowers and herbs as a symbol of the purity of Mary's whole life.

Just as the attention is being paid to the end of the Theotokos' holy life on Earth, the extreme joy at the birth of her heavenly life enters center stage!

Jesus descends to Earth, robed in his heavenly glory to escort Mary's soul directly to Heaven to begin her glorious eternal life. Her soul is represented by the image of the infant held in Jesus' arms. This image is also reminiscent of Jesus at His nativity and a reminder of His purpose for us as the Word of God. Jesus is surrounded with a blue mandorla which is flanked by two angels robed in blue. Above Jesus is a Seraphim, the highest order of angel which is six-winged and red, appearing to be on fire with Godly zeal.

Just as we need Mary's divine intercession for entry into Heaven, Mary needed Jesus' intercession for her own ascension. If we imitate the holy life of Mary full of joy, reverence, obedience and love, we too can join the angels in heavenly paradise. For the faithful, our human death is not just an end, but also a glorious beginning!

The Protection of the Theotokos (October 1)

This icon, the Protection of the Theotokos, tells the dramatic story of the event which occurred on October 1, 911 in the Blanchernae Church in Constantinople (now Istanbul) where a relic of The Virgin Mary's veil was kept. The city of Constantinople was under military threat at the time. Because it was feared the church would be destroyed, there was an all-night vigil with the faithful deep in prayer. At four o'clock in the morning St. Andrew, the Fool for Christ, saw an awesome vision of the ever virgin Mary, the Theotokos, who appeared inside the church, accompanied by St. John the Baptist, other saints and a host of angels. Mary proceeded to the front of the church, knelt down in prayer for her son's intercession for a very long time, weeping for the faithful. Then she rose above the people, removed her veil and stretched it out overhead as if covering all who were inside the church.

Upon seeing this, St. Andrew turned to his disciple, St. Epiphanius, asking, "Do you see the Queen and Lady of all is praying for the whole world?" And he had. Miraculously, the military threat was averted. The Church was saved and the people of Constantinople were spared the bloodshed and suffering.

This icon visually tells this story in a symmetrically poetic manner. The Theotokos is shown in the center floating above the Royal Doors on a series of tiny clouds in the upright position with her hands lifted in prayer. Above her is the red scarf indicating both her outstretched veil of protection and also indicating this is an indoor scene. The veil is lifted with the help of two angels, meant to represent the host of angels which had accompanied Mary. Above her veil is Jesus, the all-powerful, who answers his mother's prayers. To the right of the Royal Doors (from the viewer's perspective) are St. Andrew and his disciple. Notice how both have their feet firmly planted on the ground. To the left of the Royal Doors are two saints, representing the saints who accompanied Mary. One is St. John the Forerunner (who is specifically mentioned as one of the saints to accompany her that morning) and the other is St. Peter of Damascus. Notice how both of these saints are shown floating above the ground. St. Peter is pictured, not because he actually accompanied

Mary that morning, but instead because of the beautiful prayer he wrote for all of us to use in prayer to the Most Holy Theotokos:

> Blessed Queen of the universe, thou knowest that we sinners have no intimacy with God whom thou hast borne.
>
> But, putting our trust in thee, through thy mediation we thy servants prostrate ourselves before the Lord: for thou canst freely approach Him since He is thy son and our God.
>
> Thus I, too, unworthy believer that I am, entreat thee, holy Queen, that I may be allowed to perceive the gifts of grace bestowed on thee and on the other saints, and to understand how thou dost display so many virtues.
>
> Simply thy giving birth to the Son of God shows that thou excellest all other beings. For He Who, as creator of all, knows all things before they come into existence, found thy womb worthy of His indwelling.

In addition to the visual telling of how the Theotokos offered protection in 911 AD, this icon is a reminder to all of us on this very day that through her intercession miracles are possible.

Three

ICONS ON THE WALLS

Our Lady of the Sign (Platytera)

The Icon of Our Lady of the Sign marks the exact moment the Holy Virgin Mary fulfills Isaiah's prophesy by accepting Archangel Gabrielle's invitation to bear the son of God. As Isaiah said, "Therefore the Lord himself will give you a sign. Behold, a virgin shall conceive and bear a son, and shall call his name Immanuel (meaning God with us)" (Isaiah 7:14).

What must she be thinking?

The Son of God is depicted at the moment of his conception over her heart. His life on Earth has begun! He is dressed in His traditional robes so that He will be clearly recognizable to us as the one true Lord. Soon the virgin's womb would become, using the Byzantine Catholic phrase, "more spacious than the Heavens."

Young, unwed Mary agreed to this pregnancy and her child was not unwanted, nor was He unplanned – but her condition would be unexplainable. And, it would change the Virgin Mary's life dramatically. Yet she knew, the life she would soon be carrying would be far more precious than her own inconveniences. Yes, there were many reasons for her expression to be troubled. Nevertheless, she accepted her maternal splendor role in the history of mankind with her hands raised in glorious prayer.

In this icon, both Mary and Jesus are fully encircled by mandorlas which symbolizes the coming together of Heaven and Earth. The mandorla also signifies no one here on Earth witnessed this mystery. This revered icon is indeed a sign that Christianity and the Savior of Mankind has indeed begun as prophesied by Isaiah!

This icon also reminds me that life begins at conception. Just as the Son of God's life began at conception, so do the lives of all of us. This is the first time in Jesus' life that an image of him bears His insignia halo which identities him as Jesus, the Son of God. His life has begun!

The Holy Trinity

In 1990, Monsignor Basil Smochko introduced me to this icon. He told me that Raisa Gorbachev, wife of Mikhail Gorbachev, the Communist Leader of the USSR during the era when religion was eliminated and religious objects were confiscated, hung this particular image in their home. Certainly it had been painted by the hand of a different iconographer, but the image represented here is the same. I have no idea what Raisa or Mikhail Gorbachev thought of this image. Did they interpret it to represent Russian history? Did they realize its religious significance? Did the artistry of the image appeal to them? Did they hang it for sentimental reasons? Was Raisa holding onto her own religion while her husband was banning it for the rest of the country? At one point, Raisa – talking about this icon – reportedly told Nancy Reagan, wife of President Ronald Reagan, the image was not religious. But it is indeed a deeply religious icon – painted in an historical time for Russia.

This image was originated by Russian Andrei Rublev in the early 1400s. It is an image of the three angel visitors of Abraham at the Oaks of Mamre describing the Holy Trinity. As the Bible tells us, three men stood in front of Abraham. Upon seeing them, Abraham says,

My lord, if I have found favor in your sight, do not pass by your servant. Let a little water be brought, and wash your feet, and rest yourselves under the tree, while I fetch a morsel of bread, that may refresh yourselves, and after that you may pass on – since you have come to your servant (Genesis 18:3-5).

I invite you to contemplate this icon for a bit by yourself to discover the symbolism.

Abraham and Sarah welcomed their visitors with their hospitality. The reward for their hospitality was to have their prayers answered with the miraculous birth of their first child.

This story of hospitality is the one Rublev chose to visualize in the mystery of the Holy Trinity: Father, Son and Holy Spirit as separate persons, yet one God. Neither Abraham nor Sarah is represented. Our focus, instead, is on the three-in-one mystery which defies our full understanding.

Rublev includes the tree, the single Oak of Mamre, to anchor this icon into the story of Abraham. The water, air and earth ground this image on Earth. Our three angels, equally important, are seated and resting under the tree.

With their classical Greek hairstyles, I'd like to think these three angels are women. But angels have no gender. And, the three visitors of Abraham were indeed men. Regardless of their gender, they are identical and indivisible. The three in one reference begins.

The angel in the center represents Jesus. The two fingers resting on the table represent that He is two in one: both fully human and fully God. This angel is dressed in the blue of Heaven and the brown of the earth with a band of gold to indicate royalty. The manner in which His robe is draped – over just one shoulder with a gold band stitching the sleeve to the body of the robe is typical of the garb of Jesus in iconography. Jesus is located at the center of the image which is also indicative of Jesus' position in Christianity. The halo, though, is not the one typically associated with Jesus because this image is known as the Old Testament trinity ... before the birth of Jesus.

We see that this center angel is looking, with apparent deference, at the angel on the left (from the viewer's standpoint). This second angel represents God the Father. The robes are blue, indicative of Heaven. The robes are not just draped over one shoulder, but are fully covering the angel and look to be made of the finest silk and illuminated from within. The angel, holding the staff with both hands – indicative of great powers, is not looking at the middle angel, but instead is looking toward the third angel. The head is not lowered.

The angel on the right represents the Holy Spirit. This third angel's hand is resting on the table, indicating an ongoing relationship with us on Earth. The eyes of this angel are also lowered as a sign of respect, focusing on the feast on the table.

The three visitors of Abraham were presented with a feast including cakes of bread, a calf, butter and milk. The single urn on the table represents their feast and also symbolizes the Holy Eucharist, inviting us to contemplate the meaning of the Eucharist for all of us.

The beauty, the symmetry, the interplay among the angels, the three separate roles of each, yet the oneness of the Holy Trinity depicts a true divine love which speaks to your head, heart and soul.

Extreme Humility

On the wall behind the icon screen above the table of the preparation for the Eucharist is – to me – one of the most moving icons of all – the Icon of Extreme Humility. At first I had a hard time looking at it for a long period of time, and after a while I have a hard time turning away from it.

Humility is so difficult in our culture where we are all taught to stand up for ourselves and our rights. Here we see Jesus Christ who submitted to the persecution and death without protest. He willingly allowed His personal human temple to be destroyed – for the good of all who followed.

Here we see His lifeless body, scarred by torture, front and center. He allowed this to happen in order to take away Adam's original sin and to save all who believe in Him from the torture of eternal damnation in Hell.

Mary has one hand on her heart and the other in prayer in silence. Beloved John, shielding his eyes from the sight, is also in silent prayer. As indicated by their smaller scale, Mary and John are of lesser importance in the meaning of this icon, but clearly portray their human grief. The image of the cross is in the background held in place by angels and the tomb in the foreground.

This icon is a depiction of St. Paul's Letter to the Philippians (Chapter 2:1-11), inviting us to imitate Christ's humility:

So if there is any encouragement in Christ, any incentive of love, any participation in the Spirit, any affection and sympathy, complete my joy by being of the same mind, having the same love, being in full accord and of one mind. Do nothing from selfishness or conceit, but in humility count others better than yourselves. Let each of you look not only to his own interests, but also to the interests of others. Have this mind among yourselves, which was in Christ Jesus, who, though he was in the form of God, did not count equality with God a thing to be grasped, but emptied himself, taking the form of a servant, being born in the likeness of men. And being found in human form he humbled himself and became obedient unto death, even death on a cross. Therefore, God has highly exalted him and bestowed on him the name which is above every name, that at the name of Jesus every knee should bow, in Heaven and on Earth and under the earth, and every tongue confess that Jesus Christ is Lord, to the glory of God the Father.

Christ the Pantocrator (Christ the Judge)

The powerful icon of Christ the Pantocrator, seated on the throne as the King of the Universe, represents Jesus on the final Judgment Day. What a gloriously haunting image this is! The Greek word for Pantocrator translates as "Ruler of All," in an active sense. Notice the book here is closed.

A related icon, Christ the Teacher, also sometimes referred to as the icon of Christ the Pantocrator, invites us to lay our sins before Christ for forgiveness to lighten their burden on our souls and to encourage us to reject sin and follow Jesus. I think of the open-book teaching icon as the complement of this Christ the Judge icon to tell the full story of our active ruler who helps us live our lives to seek entry into Heaven.

This closed-book image conveys the final judgment day message to remind us that our own death may occur at any time and that we will be judged based on all we have done and failed to do. Even what we have done in darkness will be revealed. Of course our sins can be forgiven. But, we must seek forgiveness before the hour of our deaths.

The closed book which Jesus, our savior and judge, is holding in his left hand is the bejeweled Gospel Book, containing the gospels of Matthew, Mark, Luke and John. But it also has a double meaning – the book of our lives and all we have done is now complete. Jesus, with His right hand, is offering us the sign of blessing.

When I look at Jesus, His large brown eyes look directly into my eyes no matter where I am in church. These eyes compel me to pray the Jesus Prayer, "Lord Jesus Christ, Son of God, have mercy on me, a sinner."

The most compelling aspect of this icon is the pair of mismatched facial expressions on Jesus' face. To me, this icon explains what Jesus was talking about when he asked, "Do you think that I have come to give peace on earth?" Perhaps even the son of God cannot accomplish that miracle. Jesus continues, "No, I tell you, but rather division" (Luke 12:51). This is the division on Judgment day.

To help you see what I am discussing, I have digitally manipulated the original face to separate each individual expression, and then mirrored the separate expressions for full facial illustrative purposes. The differences are subtle, but significant.

The Well-Pleased Expression   **The Just Judge Expression**

The facial expression on the side of the closed book (the right-side image with two blue shoulders), is said to be the expression you will see if you are judged unfit to enter the pearly gates. This expression exclaims to me, "Look what you have done!" with eyebrows raised, eyes open wide, nostrils flared and enlarged lower lip. The gravity of the sins sinks right down through His squared-off jaw and thick neck right down to His heart. This is the expression of the just judge, who is fully robed as any judge today may be. Jesus teaches us to imitate Him in all manner of our lives except for his role as judge. In fact He teaches us not to judge one another lest we be judged. This face is the joyless face which must sentence one to an eternity of torment with fire and brimstone.

The facial expression on the side with the blessing hand (the left-side image), is said to the expression you will see if Jesus is well pleased with you. In contrast to the other side, you see how comparatively up-lifted the image is with the face almost in the shape of a heart. This is the expression of the loving face which will grant one entry through the pearly gates. The eyes are still discerning, for the many times we fell short. (The halo on the well-pleased expression appears smaller because the halo in the icon is centered on the outline of the hair and not centered on the center of the face.)

This icon reminds us that it is through Jesus that the doors to paradise will be either opened or closed. This is the image that reminds us all to both fear God and to give God glory.

The Call of St. Andrew

Shortly after Jesus began preaching in Galilee at the age of 32, just after His baptism by John, Jesus began to call His disciples, the first of whom was Andrew. The Gospel of John (1:35-40) gives us the title of this icon. John's recount of Jesus' first disciples names Andrew as the first. Andrew immediately recognized Jesus as the Messiah, and because of this he followed Jesus and later, brought his brother to Jesus. Andrew, here, is dressed in a green tunic with his hand waving to Jesus and capturing the expression in his eyes at the moment of this recognition.

The Gospels of Matthew and Mark tell it differently, with Andrew and his brother Simon (called Peter) fishing together when called by Jesus (Matt 4:20, Mark 1:18). These recounts give us the image of Jesus with arm outstretched calling the two fishermen from shore.

The Gospel of Luke provides more detail (Luke 5:2-11). The fishermen had worked all night fishing unsuccessfully and were on the shore cleaning their nets. At this point, Jesus gets into Simon Peter's boat and calls both to return to fishing – which they dutifully do. This time, they catch so much they can barely haul it all in! This Gospel gives us the image of the fish in the net.

Isn't this just like humans to all describe the same event from different points of view! And, the artistry of the icon depicts all three at once to illustrate how Jesus turned seemingly ordinary fishermen into great "fishers of men" who we still remember today.

The calling of the first disciples occurred along the northwest shore of the Sea of Galilee near the city of Gennesaret, which is fed by the Jordan River. The topography of the Sea is surrounded by hilly mounts, as abstractly presented here. While there are no notable islands in the lake, the image of the mounts add to the beauty and balance of this composition.

Martyred Byzantine Catholic Bishops

As a child, through my young adulthood, I recall the weekly prayers and petitions for religious freedom in the USSR. This icon remembers the Byzantine Catholic Bishops martyred during this period in the 20th century Soviet persecution of Christians. When this icon was completed in 2013, we all had a tendency to think about the Christian Martyrs as men and women who lived many centuries ago, but in reality there are far too many modern day martyrs.

You will notice this icon is written in a more realistic style. This is typically the case when icons are written of contemporary figures due to the prevalence of photographic images. While these Bishops are clearly recognizable, the images still conform to the priciples of iconography with elongated proportions, small mouths, large ears and broad foreheads.

The details of the lives of these martyrs are presented in the Byzantine Leaflet Series of the Byzantine Seminary Press, from which I only relay a few scant details.

Bishops Theodore and Alexander (top and bottom images) lived in the Carpathian lowland region which changed hands several times leading up to its incorporation into Soviet Ukraine in 1945; and with it, Soviet atheistic rule. Bishops Paul and Basil (left and right images) lived in Czechoslovakia when the Soviets came into power in 1948. All four remained faithful to Christ to the end, despite their persecution.

Bishop Theodore Romzha (1911 - 1947, beatified 6/27/2001) was assassinated at the age of 36. For years, Bishop Theodore enthusiastically protected the faithful and courageously refused to be intimidated by the Soviets. The Soviets, realizing they could not intimidate him into submission, staged an accident which they thought would surely kill him. When he survived, they poisoned him in his hospital bed. Research discovered that Theodore's murder was personally ordered by Nikita Khrushchev.

Bishop Alexander Chira (1897 – 1983, beatification pending), knowing full well the fate of Theodore, fearlessly succeeded him, and also became a victim of extreme soviet persecution. In 1949, he was accused of being a "traitor of the Soviet Union" and served 6 years in a Siberian concentration camp before being released. But Alexander's freedom was short-lived. The next year he was again apprehended for continuing his pastoral work and was sentenced to five years of forced labor; after which he was required to live in exile.

Even in exile he continued his underground ministry under extreme duress until Soviet law was changed to permit open religious observances. After such a long period of religious persecution, I was personally quite surprised that any religious leaders survived the Communist assault. But, Alexander did!

After helping to rebuild the Byzantine Catholic faith in the region, he died of natural causes at the age of 86.

Bishop Paul Gojdich (1888 – 1960, beatified 11/4/2001), was imprisoned in 1950 in order to pave the way for the Soviets to liquidate his Eparchy. Before this happened though, Bishop Paul was able to prepare his faithful for what was to come, encouraging them to keep their faith.

While imprisoned, the Soviets moved him from prison to prison so his people would not know where their bishop was locked up. But they always found out and came in, "procession to pray for their saintly bishop."

Throughout his imprisonment, which included long interrogations and torture, Paul remained a valiant confessor of the faith.

Bishop Basil Hopko (1904 – 1976, beatified 9/14/2003), the auxiliary Bishop to Paul, also helped prepare the Eparchy for the worst. For this, he was imprisoned along with Paul. Basil's torture consisted of first, being locked up alone in a dark cell where he completely lost track of time. Then, being forced to walk without rest for 122 consecutive days. He, too, was moved from prison to prison.

Basil's imprisonment took a heavy toll on his mental health sending him into the depths of depression in 1963. As a result he was eventually sent to a home for the aged, but not permitted to return home. There, he was nicknamed, "Our Golden Man" for his kindness and spiritual assistance. His postmortem examination revealed he had been slowly poisoned by arsenic.

These four souls of faith, and countless before and since, have known that seeking eternal splendor in Heaven is worth accepting their Earthly struggles. They did their best until their end to spread their faith with others. This icon celebrates the faith of these bishops and the fact that the strong-armed religious persecution in the former Soviet Union could not break the faith of its Christians.

The Myrrh Bearing Women

Of all the icons in St. Mary, this one intrigues me the most. This icon depicts the daybreak discovery that our Lord is no longer in His tomb, by the women who had arrived to tend to His burial needs. We know this icon is more about the women than Jesus by the relative size of the women to the wrappings in the tomb. So much of the focus surrounding the life of Jesus is on the Apostles. So, why was it that Jesus' rising on the third day was discovered by the women?

The Icon of the Myrrh Bearing Women celebrates women's place in history as the first witness of the risen Jesus – and the central role of women in the formation of the church. The story of this icon is one of love and devotion; deep sadness and great joy. All of these women: Mary the Mother of God with her three stars, Mary Magdalene with her flowing red hair, along with Martha, Susanna, Salome, Joanna, and those whose names are unknown; were loving followers of Jesus who traveled with Him and the others caring for their needs during their travels.

These women were at the back of the crowd just two days earlier when the crowd demanded the Roman Empire to "Crucify Him!" They walked with Him as he carried His cross to the Garden of Gethsemane. And they watched Him take his last breath and remained there until Joseph of Arimathea came to take His body to the freshly hewn tomb. There, the women quickly prepared His body for burial. But there was no time to complete all their preparations as the Sun was setting and their Jewish observance of Passover must begin. Their final task, anointing the body with Myrrh, was postponed until sunrise on Sunday, where this scene takes place.

The women must have approached the tomb with great sorrow and a sense of finality to perform this last act of caring for our Lord. Each woman brought an urn filled with the carefully prepared contents, only to find out that their beloved was nowhere to be found. They must have thought the Romans had taken His body. But, why the Romans would remove His shroud was unknown – until they finally realized He had risen.

The risen Christ showed himself to Mary Magdalene before all others. After the women and also the disciples (who had heard from the women that His tomb was empty) had gone home, she lingered at the tomb weeping. The story is told in John 10, 11-18:

> Mary stood weeping outside the tomb, and as she wept she stooped to look into the tomb; and she saw two angels in white, sitting where the body of Jesus had lain, one at the head and one at the feet. They said to her, "Woman, why are you weeping?" She said to them, "Because they have taken away my lord, and I do not know where they have laid him." Saying this, she turned round and saw Jesus standing, but she did not know that it was Jesus. Jesus said to her, "Woman, why are you weeping? Whom do you seek?" Supposing him to be the gardener she said to him, "Sir, if you have carried him away, tell me where you have laid him, and I will take him away." Jesus said to her, "Mary." She turned and said to him in Hebrew, "Rabboni!" (which means Teacher). Jesus said to her, "Do not hold me, for I have not ascended to the Father; but go to my brethren and say to them, I am ascending to my Father and your Father, to my God and your God."

What an incredible turn of events! From weeping for his passing and for being unable to pay proper respects for His missing body, to realizing that His body needs no burial tending at all and He lives on! What joy she must feel! He had risen on the *third day* just as He had taught! And, Mary Magdalene was the messenger of the good news!

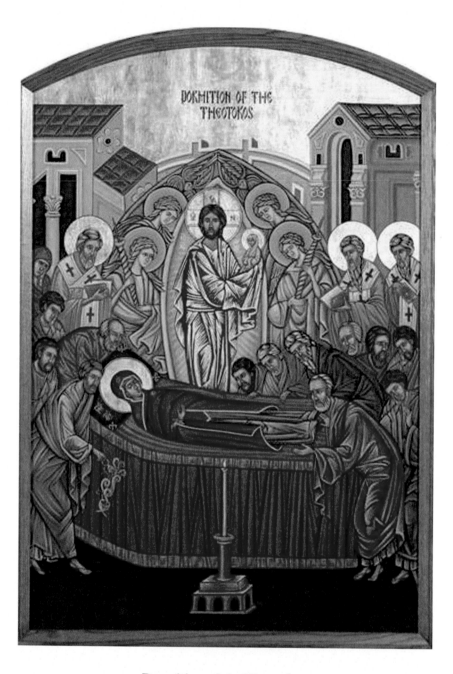

Dormition of the Theotokos

This is the second icon of the Dormition of the Theotokos, the hopeful icon that all of our souls *can* be born again and brought to Heaven, which is depicted inside St. Mary. This is a good icon to discuss as our final icon in this book because it is the icon which this particular church is dedicated. These two icon of the mystery of salvation illustrate how the same icon can be interpreted differently by the hand of a different iconographer.

The similarities are striking: Mary, the Theotokos, on her deathbed surrounded by the now aged apostles; several bishops; and Jesus – surrounded by a mandorla with angels – carrying Mary's soul straight to Heaven. This particular dormition icon on the wall contains more details because the image is much larger than the one on the icon screen and also is closer to the eye of the viewer. The composition differs in part due to the difference in the proportions on the image, and in part out of the inspired-by-God artistic interpretation.

Iconographers pray and fast during the design and painting phases of producing an icon in order to allow the Holy Spirit to inspire the mind and hand of the iconographer to tell the story of the icon. Notice how the style of both conforms to traditional Byzantine principles with the otherworldly-proportioned bodies, reverse perspective and symmetry to reflect the transfigured state of the subjects on Earth as if in Heaven.

I hope the theme of this icon – that you can be lifted up to Heaven at the end of your Earthly life – is the feeling this book leaves you with. Just as Mary is surrounded by angels and saints, we, too, can be surrounded by them in prayer to help us along our individual paths on Earth.

Conclusion

I n conclusion, it is my hope that the exquisite beauty of the icons inside St. Mary in the village of Marblehead, Ohio can serve you in your own meditations as they have for my spiritual journey in writing this book. I encourage you to invite the windows into Heaven into your heart, mind and soul.

I took on this project to honor my father, who died at age 88 as a result of an accident. When it became obvious he would not recover from his injuries, I told him a story from my childhood when I did not recognize him. I must have been about three years old.

At that time, I had never before spoken to my father on the phone, but I answered the phone that day when he called to speak to my mother. I did not recognize his voice, but he spoke to me in a very familiar manner (which I did not like because I had been taught not to speak to strangers), and he asked to speak to my mother. Despite my dismay by his conversation, I obediently found my mother in the backyard where she was playing with my brother and announced, "Mom, there is some strange man on the phone who wants to talk to you."

When I later found out the "strange" man on the other end of the phone line was my own father, I was shocked that I did not recognize the man I loved so dearly. The experience changed my outlook on life that day. What I thought was strange, was a result of _my_ ignorance and not the situation itself.

I retold this story to my father on his deathbed in hopes that he would come to me after his death; and if he did, that I would be open to the new experience and be able to recognize him.

The night after he died I believe my father's spirit did come to me. I cannot tell if it was a truly otherworldly experience or merely a vivid dream. But I can attest to the fact that because of this experience, I had no reason to grieve for his death.

That night, I was awakened from a sound sleep by a feeling that the spirit of my father was there in my bedroom trying to communicate with me. His spirit looked like a glowing sphere of shimmering luminous gold. I felt it was unmistakably my father although there was nothing I can describe as familiar other than the essence that was unmistakably his. The experience, as I recall, involved either no words at all, or so many words all at one time that no individual words were discernible. Yet, his glorious message was indelibly scribed on my soul! He was so overjoyed he was unquestionably giddy! He exuded so much love, the height of which I had never imagined possible. I cannot find the words to describe his awesome message, nevertheless I perceived he was telling me how incredibly wonderful it was for him in the afterlife!

After he left me, I drifted back to sleep blissfully knowing Dad had been royally welcomed into Heaven – a Heaven that is far better than I had ever dared to imagine!

I believe my father came to me that night to give me a glimpse of Heaven and to share his new experience! Whether my encounter with his spirit was real or not, adequately comprehended or not, its impact on my life is undeniable! Now when I reflect on what I learned from my dear dad that night, I am convinced that the divine icons at St. Mary truly provide windows into Heaven! Yet, relative to my experience with my father, these exquisite images have their limitations.

Truly, how do humans express the inexpressible? Heaven is far better than earthly images can fully express. I am certain my understanding of these icons is incomplete and that I (and you) will learn much more through continued prayer and meditation. You do not need to be Byzantine Catholic to learn from these Byzantine Icons.

If you find yourself in the vicinity of Marblehead, Ohio, I invite you to join us for liturgy. We still follow many of the ancient liturgical traditions of early Christians. Both Roman Catholics and Orthodox Christians who are in good standing to receive communion at their home church are invited to receive Holy Communion with us to satisfy your weekly obligation.

Appendix 1:
Writing Icons

As a part of my preparation for writing this book, I took two icon writing classes under the direction of Father Marek Visnovsky. Although icons can be written on any surface, our class was based on the tradition of painting icons on a board already prepared to accept the paint. The process of painting an icon is in and of itself a transformative religious experience.

We started with a smooth wooden board which represents the cross itself. But, the grain of the wood, without additional preparation would provide an inadequate surface to preserve the icon for generations to come. So, the wood surface is prepared with linen and gesso. The linen covering the wood represents the linen Jesus was wrapped in following His crucifixion. The gesso represents the stone of His tomb. The process of metamorphosis has begun and will be accomplished with each individual brush stroke.

The raw materials used to produce icons represent the four kingdoms of our world coming together: mineral, vegetable, animal, and human. The mineral kingdom provides some of the pigments of the paint, the vegetable kingdom provides the living wood and other paint pigments; the animal kingdom provides the brushes; and the human kingdom provides the labor. All four are being transformed, or figuratively resurrected, in the process of creating the icon as a reflection of God.

Kay Zekany

The process of creating an icon is actually an active form of prayer. We start with the raw materials and an image which we strive to create; an image which has been designed over the centuries with the purpose of creating a visual telling of scripture. This is not to say that new icons cannot be designed today, but those which are, are designed following the ancient traditions and imagery. We begin work on the icon with a prayer. With each subsequent brush stroke we seek to imitate and represent the saintly figures with the aid of God. In this way, God is using us as an instrument to create these beautiful images. Because God is working through us, our hand is just writing what God has created through the iconographer.

We start by painting the dark colors before adding the lighter colors, the dull before the bright because this is how God sees us. Before we know of God, we are in darkness, and the more we know of God the more He brings the light of His wisdom into our lives. In this manner, the iconographer brings the light into the World!

Appendix 2: History of St. Mary

St. Mary Byzantine Catholic Church was started by Carpatho-Russian families from Austria-Hungary (now Slovakia) who were drawn to the area to work in the local limestone quarry which is still in operation today. The parent church to St. Mary was the Greek Catholic Church on Kelley's Island, which has long since been raised. In particular Mr. George Gulick, a member of the Kelley's Island parish, moved his family to Marblehead in 1892 and happily found many families of his countrymen already living in the Marblehead area – some of whom banded together to form this church. The founding fathers of this church, primarily quarrymen, include George Boytim, John Dziak, George Gulick, Michael Hitraly, John Juby and Michael Sotak. This parish was officially established as a congregation in 1897.

The parish founders were hard-working, honest, God-fearing and loving people who had been a part of the European peasantry. They came to this country with a hope and a dream to experience the freedom and opportunity to prosper in this new country: America. Mr. George Boytim, owner of the local grocery and dry goods store, is credited with helping his fellow parishioners with money management. He was also largely responsible for St. Mary purchasing their original parish properties.

The first church was a small wooden structure on Main Street which was destroyed by fire. In 1904, a new church was built on the same foundation and blessed by Bishop I. F. Horstmann, the Roman Catholic Bishop from Cleveland who helped the region's Eastern-rite Catholic churches who had no bishop at the time in the United States.

St. Mary Church, while always under the Pope, has not always been referred to as a Byzantine Catholic Church. It was originally known as a Greek Catholic Church. But as trends in names go, the name Greek was replaced by Byzantine – perhaps to distinguish it from Orthodox Christian Churches which are not associated with the Pope and the Roman Catholic Church.

While the white clapboard church, which once stood adjacent to the cemetery property on Main Street, served the parish well, an opportunity arose to purchase the waterfront property adjacent to the lighthouse at a modest price. Mrs. Biro, who owned the property, lived next door to our current parish property. This was at a time when the area waterfront was becoming popular for tourists and she feared a future of living next door to a condominium complex, which prompted her to consider who she would want as her ideal neighbor. Her conclusion was that it should be a church. So, she first offered the property to her own church, St. Joseph's Roman Catholic Church in Marblehead. But they declined. So, she took her offer next to Fr. Frank Korba, St. Mary Parish pastor at the time, who accepted her gracious offer.

The property was purchased in 1973 and the decision was made to construct the new church. Construction began in 1975. The first Divine Liturgy was performed on Christmas Eve 1976 by Fr. Korba with full, standing room only congregation in attendance. The church was officially dedicated on Sunday April 24, 1977. The church social hall was built from 1983 - 1985.

As the 1997 100th Year Parish Anniversary celebration booklet says, "The first one hundred years at St. Mary Byzantine Catholic Parish in Marblehead has been very rewarding for this little religious village and we look forward to a blessed future."

Appendix 3:
Icon Dedications
(listed in the order discussed in this book)

- **Christ the Teacher** – In memory of Frank and Lillian Kopchak by Miss Margaret Kopchak
- **Mother of God** – In memory of Mike and Mary Kopchak by Miss Mary Kopchak
- **Holy John, the Forerunner of The Lord** – In memory of Clara Capko by Joseph Capko
- **Our Holy Father Nicholas, Wonderworker of Myra** – By Mr. and Mrs. Richard Kmetz Family
- **The Royal Doors** (Four Evangelists: Sts. Matthew, John, Mark and Luke) – In memory of Anna Boytim by Steve and Mildred Boytim
- **The Holy Deacon Phillip** – By Fr. Edmund Jadwisiak
- **The Holy Deacon and Protomartyr Stephen** – By Ladies Lodge, Greek Catholic Union #504
- **The Risen Christ** – In memory of the John Richick Family
- **The Nativity of Christ** - In memory of the John Batcha Family
- **The Birth of the Theotokos** – By Mr. and Mrs. Peter Boytim Family
- **The Entrance of the Theotokos into the Temple** – By Mr. and Mrs. Milliard Snider and Family

- **The Annunciation** – By Casmir Jadwisiak Family
- **The Presentation of the Lord** – By Mr. and Mrs. Andrew Zura
- **The Theophany of the Lord** – By Mr. and Mrs. Steve Meterko
- **The Transfiguration of the Lord** – By Mr. and Mrs. Emil Batcha and John
- **The Entrance into Jerusalem** – By John Krynock Family
- **The Mystical Supper** – In memory of Mr. and Mrs. George Monak, Sr., and Mr. and Mrs. Michael J. Dziak, Sr. by Mr. and Mrs. Daniel Monak Family
- **The Crucifixion of the Lord** – By Mr. and Mrs. Allan Shrock and Bryan
- **The Ascension of the Lord** – By the Luska Family
- **The Descent of the Holy Spirit** – By Mr. and Mrs. George Ihnat
- **The Dormition of the Theotokos** – In memory of the desceased members of the Monak and Frania Families, the deceased members of the Dziak and Capko Families and Daniel Quilty by Mr. and Mrs. Daniel Monak Family
- **The Protection of the Theotokos** – In memory of George and Julia Elchisko and Mary Pipas
- **The Call of St. Andrew** – In memory of Andy Zekany, Jr. by Family and Friends
- **Martyred Byzantine Catholic Bishops** – In memory of Fr. Edmund Jadwisiak
- **The Myrrh Bearing Women** – Anonymous
- **Dormition of the Theotokos** – By Fr. Bryan Eyman and Family in memory of the Grandparents

Please note: Unfortunately the dedications for Our Lady of the Sign, The Holy Trinity, Extreme Humility and Christ the Pantocrator have become a piece of lost church history. None of the current members of the parish can recall who dedicated these fine works to our church. As this information is revealed, proper acknowledgement will be made in future editions of this book.

Appendix 4: Glossary

Eparchy – is comparable to a diocese in that it is a collection of parishes which is governed by a bishop.

Iconographer – one who writes or paints an icon.

Mandorla – is the blue "circle" or "almond-shaped" aureole of light encircling Jesus or the Virgin Mary which indicates the coming together of Heaven on Earth. It is seen in the following icons: The Risen Christ, The Ascension of the Lord, The Dormition of the Theotokos, Our Lady of the Sign, Christ the Pantocrator. It represents Heaven on Earth, unseen by human eyes.

Omophorion – is the distinctive long, broad stole worn by an eastern Christian bishop which is intricately draped over the shoulders and has crosses embroidered to be draped symmetrically on a bishop's shoulders to come together at the front. You see it in the following icons in this book: Our Holy Father Nicholas, Wonderworker of Myra, The Dormition of the Theotokos, and Martyred Byzantine Catholic Bishops.

Pantocrator – The role of Jesus Christ as the "Ruler of All" in the universe. The icon of Christ the Pantocrator depicts Jesus separating those who will spend eternity in Heaven and those condemned to eternity in Hell.

Pascha – another term for Easter.

Theophany – another term for Epiphany.

Theotokos – is the title given to Mary the Mother of God which means that we recognize her as the one who gave birth to God.

Appendix 5: Further Readings on this Subject

I consulted many individuals and sources in the preparation and writing of this book including church archives and talking to current and former priests. The written sources which provided the most influence on this book are listed below. In addition to the books and web resources listed below, good general information on icons can be found online at both Wikipedia and OrthodoxWiki.

Reference:
Bible, The Ignatius Bible, Revised Standard Version, Second Catholic Edition, 2002, Ignatius Press, San Francisco.

Influential Readings:
Eternal Word Television Network, *Mary in Scripture*. Retrieved from http://www.ewtn.com/library/MARY/MARYINSC.HTM.

Matthewes-Green, Frederica, *The Open Door: Entering the Sanctuary of Icons and Prayer*, 2003, Paraclete Press, Brewster, Massachusetts.

Matthewes-Green, Frederica, *The Lost Gospel of Mary: The Mother of Jesus in Three Ancient Texts*, 2007, Paraclete Press, Brewster, Massachusetts.

Martin, Lynette, Sacred Doorways: A Beginners Guide to Icons, Paraclete Press, Brewster, Massachusetts, 2002.

Martyred Carpatho-Rusyn Byzantine Catholic Bishops, Byzantine Leaflet Series of the Byzantine Seminary Press. Retrieved from http://www.carpatho-rusyn.org/spirit/.

Ouspensky, L., Lossky, V. Translated by Palmer, G.E. H., Kadloubovsky E., *The Meaning of Icons*, 1999, St Vladimir's Seminary Press, Chrestwod, N.Y..

Persson, Ann. *The Circle of Love: Praying with Rublev's Icon of the Trinity*, 2011, The Bible Reading Fellowship, Abingdon, Oxford, UK,.

Solrunn, Nes, *The Mystical Language of Icons*, William B. Eerdmans Publishing Company, Grand Rapids, Michigan, Second Edition, 2004.

Walker, A., Translator from Ante-Nicene Fathers, Vol. 8. Edited by Alexander Roberts, James Donaldson, and A. Cleveland Coxe. (Buffalo, NY: Christian Literature Publishing Co., 1886.) Revised and edited for New Advent by Kevin Knight. *The Protoevangelium of James*. Retrieved from http://www.newadvent.org/fathers/0847.htm.

Weitzman, K., Alibeqasvili, G, Volskaja, A., Chatzidakis, M., Babic, G., Alpatov, M., Voinescu, T. *The Icon*, English Edition translated by Mondadori, A., London, Studios Editions, Ltd., 1990.

Williams, Rowan, *Ponder These Things: Praying with Icons of the Virgin*, Paraclete Press, Brewster, Massachusetts, 2012.

Appendix 6:
About the Author

Kay Zekany, Ph.D. is the author of numerous academic and professional publications, including educational materials which have been used world-wide. She is a passionate college professor and Christian who spent over four years composing this book to pay tribute to the legacy of her father, Andy Zekany, Jr., who was a lifelong member of St. Mary and physically built the church along his crew.

This is her first foray into writing about her faith. In doing so, she combines her two life mottos: "Life should be divine," and "I help others achieve their dreams."

Kay lives with her husband, Dan, of 25 years and their golden retriever, Ginger. They split their time between their condo in Port Clinton, Ohio and home in Lake Charles, Louisiana.

Made in the USA
Middletown, DE
10 July 2015